GW00500244

Lady Maclean's
Cook Book

Collins

Revised edition 1966
Reprinted 1967
Reprinted 1968
Reprinted 1970
This Edition 1973
Reprinted 1984

Maclean, Veronica, *Lady*
    Lady Maclean's cook book.—[3rd ed] repr.
    1. Cooking
    I. Title
641.5   TX717

ISBN 0 00 211453 4

© Veronica Maclean 1965

Made and printed in Great Britain
William Collins Sons & Co Ltd, Glasgow

Sir Fitzroy and Lady Maclean.

Before and After.

When I married, I weighed ten stone. Now I weigh fifteen. Need I say more?

Fitzroy Maclean.

Contents

Introduction   7

Soups   13

Hot First Course or Supper Dishes   29

Cold First Course or Supper Dishes   53

Hors d'Oeuvres   64

Poultry and Game   69

Fish   89

Meat   111

Puddings - cold   143

Puddings - hot   173

Scones and Cakes   191

Savouries   209

Odds and Ends   217

English and American Equivalent Measures   227

Index   228

I dedicate these pages
to
Mrs . Cockerill
who taught me to cook
but
who fortunately knows
she will always do it better herself

Introduction

Towards the end of the Eighteenth Century my husband's great-great-grandmother, Lady Margaret Maclean of Ardgour, started keeping in a neat copperplate hand a large quarto book in which she recorded her favourite recipes and the names of the friends who had given them to her.

Not long ago I decided to do the same and this is the result. It is my own very personal scrap-book, collected from family recipes of several generations, both Scottish and English; from my travels round the world in my husband's wake; and from my friends whose food I particularly admire. I would like to thank them all for their generosity in not only parting with so many succulent secrets but also in letting me publish them.

Some of our recipes may be too complicated or extravagant for everyday use, and these are for special occasions - others are perfectly adaptable to the world we live in; but on the whole these recipes represent, I hope, Family or Country-house cooking at its best as opposed to Classical, Restaurant, or Grand London Food.

Grand Country-house cooking has pretty well come to an end.   It probably reached its most dazzling heights with the Edwardians, in those great shooting and week-long house parties before the First War, when forty people would often sit down to luncheon or dinner, catered for, it is the only word, by a small army of professionals and their apprentices behind the ever swinging baize doors.

But good food, even then, was not all on a Rothschild scale. There were many famous hostesses who disliked ostentation and genuinely preferred simple food, perfectly cooked, whose country quality was evident.   It was often less classically French, but it was a great deal more original and individual, and gave them much more creative scope.

It is to these progenitors of modern good cooking and to their descendants that this collection owes so much, for their recipes really started an era as well as ending one.

Lady Jekyll, my favourite Edwardian trend-setter, was the doyenne of them all, and I include several of her recipes with the generous permission of her daughter, Lady Freyberg, who I hope will soon re-publish the whole wonderful collection of "Kitchen Essays." Others have come to me directly and indirectly through her sister, Lady Horner.   Mells food during her reign (and Mrs. Goulds') was something never to be forgotten.

Lady Moyra Cavendish was also an inspired hostess, and
Holker food was perhaps the subtlest and most original of all.
She is represented here by her daughter, Mrs. Campbell-Gray,
her two grand-daughters-in-law, Lady Cranborne and Lady Amabel
Lindsay, and the Duchess of Devonshire.

Lady Lindley, my aunt, enjoyed the advantages of
Diplomatic life for recipe-collecting all over the world.
In America diplomats are aptly called "cooky-pushers" and
certainly Ambassadresses I have known have always been mines
of gastronomic information.   Sometimes their recipes are a
little grand, but fortunately my aunt was not.   Some Beaufort
recipes originate from her, and her daughters, Lady McEwen,
Lady Hardwicke and Mrs. Keswick have all sent me recipes.

Lastly I must pay tribute to Beaufort food, on which I
was nurtured, and to the food in Florence on which I was
educated; to my mother-in-law Mrs. Charles Maclean, and to
my mother, Laura Lovat, or Lady Love-at-First-Sight, as an
admirer once called her, munching, no doubt, on some delicious
delicacy at the time.   On her mother's side she was a Tennant,
which half explains her wide knowledge and love of good food -
though how that garrulous family ever stopped talking long
enough to eat, I often wonder.   Like most of her generation
she could not boil an egg herself, but she knew by instinct

and experience exactly how food should taste, and was always able to impart this knowledge to others. She was admirably aided and sustained by three wonderful cooks, Mrs. Grady, Miss Alice Donnelly, and Miss Joan Matheson. And now my sister-in-law, Rosie Lovat, has not only carried on the Beaufort tradition but enriched it, as will be seen by the many contributions she has made to this book.

On my own behalf I should like to thank Miss Rosemary Hume, of the Cordon Bleu School of Cookery, and Mrs. Elizabeth David, of "French Country Cooking", both of whose recipes I have used so often that I rather unforgiveably think of them as my own. They are the Living Prophets to whom I always turn when in doubt.

And finally I would like to thank Mrs. Young, of Portsonachan, for all her delicious recipes, but particularly for Norwegian "Dilled" Salmon, which is nicer than smoked salmon and for the preparation of which a Spring sowing of Dill is imperative and should immediately be planned.

V. M.

Strachur

July 1966

Section headings are designed by Avril V. Gibb.

Lady Anne Hope
1792

TO MAKE AN OLIO

Take of the best Yellow Turnips and Orange
Carrots the same quantity, cut into Dices; two or
three Onions cut small; six white Cabbage Lettuces;
two stalks of Celery and a few Artichoke Buttons; a
little Parsley and Cauliflower and a few young Pease.
Take a small bit of Ham and 2 ounces of Butter, put
all into a Stew Pan and cover it close that none of
the steam may get out. Put it on a slow fire - it
should stew 4 or 5 hours - a little before it is
dished put in two cloves and a little Salt and Pepper
and half a pint of good gravy.

Observe there is no water put to it and if carefully done it is as good without the Gravy.

*   *   *

This is a receipt from Lady Margaret's cookery book which is
not so confusing as most - having no isinglass to chip or
purees to put through hair sieves, or mutchkins or hogsheads
to measure. Qute a few of the recipes are "strengthening"
jellys or soups, which must have been much in demand. And
small wonder! There is also a receipt for dyeing pink muslin
from Lady Haddington and one called "Lord Ponsonby's Recipe
for Cholera".

NOTE

The reader will not always find in these recipes ingredients
measured to the very last quarter ounce and the words "to
taste" occur rather more often than they do in most cookery
books. This is because they are mostly "handed-down"
recipes and can bear slight alterations and variations,
according to the taste of the cook or her employer, (the
two being usually one and the same in 1966.)

I am always tasting, criticising and improving on every dish
I cook, whether old or new, and I advise my readers to do
likewise, for when a cook stops tasting, and putting her own
individual feeling and imagination into her food, it soon
becomes dull and ordinary.

All recipes in this book are designed to feed from five to
six greedy people, unless otherwise stated.

Soups.

Torbreck Farm House, Scaniport,
Inverness-shire.

MAGGIE'S OYSTER STEW

1 pint fresh or tinned oysters   2 onions
1 pint cream   butter
1 tablespoonful sherry

    One pint of oysters to a pint of cream.
(If this is found to be too rich a little milk
can be used with less cream, to thin it down).
2 onions chopped and sweated in butter till
golden.   Chop half the oysters and add the onion,
cook gently for 10 minutes.   Add the rest of the
oysters whole and the cream.   Bring to the boil
but do not let boil.   Add a tablespoonful of
sherry at the last moment before serving.

This dish is very good made with tinned
oysters if fresh ones cannot be obtained.

Colonel Michael Dunning-White.

LEEK AND POTATO SOUP (POTAGE PARMENTIER)

1 lb. potatoes	2 egg-yolks
2 leeks	Little milk or cream
small piece butter	croutons of fried bread

Peel a pound of potatoes and cut them in quarters. Cut the white part of three leeks into thin slices and sweat gently in a little butter until golden.   Add the potatoes, and a pint and a half of hot water.   Season with salt, put on the lid, bring to the boil and boil quickly for twenty minutes or so.   When the potatoes are soft, pass through a wire sieve, rinse the saucepan, put the puree back into it, bring to the boil and simmer gently for five minutes. Correct the seasoning, adding pepper, take the pan off the fire, stir in two egg-yolks beaten up with a little milk or cream, and add at the last a small piece of butter.   Serve very hot, with croutons of fried bread.

Fish Soup -

Three good sized haddocks.
Lay aside the best parts of two
and boil as stock the rest of the
fish head bones etc for 2 hours with
an onion and savoury herbs.
Skim and strain. Thicken with a very
little flour butter & cream & season
with pepper and a little cayenne.
Add the pieces of fish and boil gently
till ready.
Just before serving add an egg well
beaton.

The Duchess of Devonshire.

GREEN PEA SOUP (PURÉE SAINT-GERMAIN)

1¼ pint shelled peas   few tablespoonfuls freshly
1 pint chicken or veal consommé   cooked peas
           few tiny leaves chervil

Boil 1¼ pint of shelled peas in salted water, and when they are
done, drain them well and pound them in a mortar.   Add a pint
of chicken or veal consomme, mix and rub through a hair sieve,
or churn in a liquidiser.   Heat up, and finish with a little butter,
garnishing with a few tablespoonfuls of freshly cooked peas, and
a few tiny leaves of chervil.

COLD PEA SOUP

Same as above but put into fridge for at least 4 hours to ice. ✗.
Instead of finishing with whole peas and chervil, put into each
soup cup or plate a few small cubes of diced cucumber, and a
pinch of chopped mint.   A little cream can also be added to make
the soup richer.

COLD PEA SOUP - QUICK VERSION

Use one packet of Batchelor's Thick Pea Soup.   Thin down with
cream and freeze. ✗ -   Not quite so good!

Really cold, but of course not frozen.
Chill is probably a better word -

Mushroom 6, ABERCORN PLACE, Soup.
N.W.8.
1 lb mushrooms CUNNINGHAM 9021. ½ pt. thin Béchamel
¾ pt Chicken Stock . A little
lemon juice, butter & cream.
(4 people)

Wash & peel mushrooms &
chop coarsely. Put in saucepan
with a little butter & cook till
tender, but without browning.
Rub through sieve & add to
the hot Béchamel Sauce; stir
over slow heat for 10 minutes. Strain
through coarse sieve & add to
the hot chicken stock - stir &
simmer for a few minutes,
season with a little lemon juice
& lastly stir in 2 or 3 tablespoons
cream.

Mrs Franz Osborn
(Miss Josephine Rüegg)

This soup is a seasonal one, but all the nicer for that, and really worth the effort. Once you have located your nettle-bed, (there are all too many in my garden), you will observe that every year in the spring a new and tender growth appears. Cut the nettles with a hand scythe while they are still young, gather with gloves, wash well and proceed with the recipe.

<u>NETTLE SOUP</u>

Blanch 2 lbs. Nettles.

Strain and press water out well.

Fry in butter in a covered stew pan.

Add 2 pints good stock.

When boiling, add 2 lbs. potatoes.

When cooked, pass through a sieve,

put back in stew pan and add some

boiling milk to bring it to the

proper thickness.

Add some cream and a little chervil

at the last minute.

Mrs. N. Lancaster.

POTAGE CRÈME MAIZE

1   Large tin Sweet Corn.
1   Tablespoonful Brown Sugar.
1   pt. Chicken Stock.
½   pt. Whipped Cream.
Salt and Pepper.

Make thin sauce with chicken stock.

Add sugar and sweet corn and cook.

Pass through sieve when ready and re-heat.

If too thick add a little more stock and

lastly cream.

———

4 persons

Mrs. Stirling of Keir
(Mrs. Alice Thomson)

TOMATO SOUP

½ PINT MILK   SALT & PEPPER

½ PINT STOCK   DASH OF LEE & PERRINS

1 LB RIPE TOMATOES (COOKED)   "   " MIXED HERBS.

1 SMALL ONION   (COOKED)

1 TEASPOON SUGAR

1 TABLESPOON BUTTER

1 TABLESPOON FLOUR

.PLACE ALL INGREDIENTS INTO BLENDER EXCEPT MILK. SWITCH TO No 12 SPEED AND RUN FOR ABOUT ONE MINUTE. PLACE IN A SAUCEPAN AND COOK SLOWLY UNTIL QUITE HOT. ADD MILK BUT DO NOT BOIL ONCE MILK HAS BEEN ADDED. WHEN SOUP IS READY PASS THROUGH A HAIR SIEVE. ADD COLOURING IF REQUIRED. SERVE WITH CHEESE CROÛTES.

CHEESE CROÛTES

1 OZ GRATED CHEESE   1-2 ROUNDS BREAD.

½ OZ BUTTER   ½" THICK

     PEPPER, SALT, MUSTARD, CAYENNE.

WORK CHEESE & BUTTER TOGETHER, SEASON. TOAST BREAD ON ONE SIDE SPREAD MIXTURE THICKLY ON THE OTHER TOAST TO A GOLDEN BROWN, CUT INTO SMALL SQUARES. SERVE AT ONCE.

Mrs. A.D. CAMERON.

Mrs. A.D. Cameron

Velouté de Chevreuil aux Marrons.

Made from left over Venison
Preferably having been served with a Purée of Chestnuts
and a Sauce Poivrade

If not unsweetened purée of chestnuts can be used
from a can, adding hot milk & butter to soften
and lighten it.

"Sauce poivrade" may be found in any classical
cook book.
It is essentially a blend, finely strained,
of the marinade used for the venison,
it's gravy
lots of freshly ground pepper
a little cream.

The soup is made simply by blending
& straining finely the left-over venison,
chestnut purée & poivrade sauce in about
3 equal parts. If too thick, thin out with
a little broth.

The Duchess of Argyll

Vichyssoise.

4 large Leeks
1 small onion
4 medium sized potatoes
Chicken stock, cream.
Mince leeks and onion, place in a
saucepan with 4 tablespoons butter
add ½ teacup water. Gently simmer
for 10-20 minutes. Add chicken
stock (1½ pints) and potatoes, simmer
½ hour. Put through with sieve
Cool. Add cream, chives. or curry
powder to taste, before serving.

Serves 4 people

Lady Amabel Lindsay

Bruern
Churchill
Oxford

WATER CRESS SOUP

4 bunches of Water Cress, $\frac{1}{2}$ tab butter.

For Veloute 1 oz. flour, 1 oz. butter, 2 pints stock, 5 egg yolks, 3 tabs double cream.

Remove leaves from the stems of water cress. Wash and drain & chop. Put in heavy saucepan with $\frac{1}{2}$ tab butter (melted) cover & allow cress to melt over very low heat for about 20 mins. Make Veloute by cooking butter & flour together slowly for a few mins. then allowing to cool. Bring stock to the boil & add the cold flour & butter mixture. Stirring it in until smooth. Bring to the boil & boil slowly for about 20 mins. Skim & add water cress. Cook slowly for about 10 mins. Season (no pepper). While the soup is cooking beat together the egg yolks & cream, then slowly beat in about 4 tabs soup. Remove soup from the heat and when it has stopped boiling stir in the cream & egg mixture very gently with a spoon. Serves 6.

The Hon. Mrs. Michael Astor

GASPACHO

A cold Spanish soup made off the fire without cooking.

1	pint cold Beef Stock.
½	tablespoonful good Italian Tomato Puree.
2	tablespoonfuls Paprika.
2	tablespoonfuls Salt.
4	ozs. Lemon Juice.
4	ozs. good Olive Oil.
1	Clove Garlic (to taste).

2	Onions.
2	lbs. Tomatoes.
2	Green Peppers.
	Cucumber.
	Bread Croutons.

Drip the olive oil into the cold bouillon beating all the time. Stir in tomato puree, paprika, lemon juice, salt, and garlic to taste. Chop all the raw vegetables fairly fine, removing seeds and skin from tomatoes and seeds and stalks from peppers (before chopping, roll peppers on hot stove to blister skins, which brings out their taste). Pour the liquid soup over the vegetables and leave in fridge for at least 4 hours. Before serving add 1 inch of peeled and diced raw cucumber and cold diced croutons of bread which have been fried in butter.

PORTSONACHAN,

BY DALMALLY,

ARGYLL.

CONSOMMÉ à l'INDIENNE

Put into a stew-pan a quart of good stock, slice
into it 2 onions, 1 large cooking apple, a tablespoonful of dessicated cocoanut, a dessertspoonful of curry
powder (or more if it is liked hot), and the carcass
of a roast chicken, rabbit or game bones, and let
simmer gently for an hour. Strain and remove the
fat, and clarify in the usual manner. Re-boil and
serve with pieces of game or chicken in the marmite,
and a very little plain boiled rice, also kept hot,
to be added into each portion as helped.

Lady Jekyll, whose "KITCHEN ESSAYS"
        will shortly be republished.

*   *   *

CLEAR BORTCHOK

3   pints clear Venison Stock.
4   Raw Beetroots.
1   gill Cream, Fresh or made sour by
            adding lemon juice.

Put the stock into a clean stew-pan and add the beetroot grated, simmer gently for 2 hours, strain, return
to pan, season, reheat and serve with whipped cream,
or sour cream.

This soup does not pretend to be like Russian Bortsch -
which is a real peasant soup, delicious, but a complete
meal in itself and not suitable for a dinner party.

Mrs. James Young

TOMATO SOUP WITH ORANGE

```
2   lbs. Tomatoes fresh or canned.
1   Medium size Carrot.
1   Medium size Onion.
1   Bay Leaf.
1   Lemon, sliced.
1   Orange, sliced.
6   Pepper corns.
2   Pints Stock, chicken or veg.
½   Pint Orange Juice.
Salt.
1½  oz. Butter.
1½  oz. Flour.
A little Sugar to taste.
1 gill of Cream and slices of Orange
                    to garnish.
```

Choose ripe Tomatoes, wipe, cut in half and squeeze
lightly to remove seeds.   Slice the onion and carrot
finely and put in a stew pan together with the tomatoes,
lemon, orange, bay leaf, pepper corns, orange juice,
and stock.   Add a little salt and simmer for about
an hour with the lid off, strain through a fine
sieve.   Rince out the pan, melt the butter in it,
add the flour, mix well and add the tomato pulp,
Simmer for 5 minutes or longer if necessary to
thicken the soup a little more, add sugar to taste.
Serve garnished with a slice of orange and a spoonful
of whipped cream.

Mrs. James Young

Hot First Course
or Supper Dishes.

Eggs with Peperonata

2 tablesps corn oil;
1 clove garlic crushed;
2 large green Peppers;
 (seeded and sliced)
4 oz bacon:
 (fat removed)
8 eggs;

1 medium sized onion;
  (finely sliced)
8 oz tomatoes;
  (skinned and sliced)
Salt;
$\frac{1}{4}$ teasp. caster sugar;
1 oz finely grated Cheddar cheese

Method

Heat the oil, add onion and garlic and cook until transparent.
Add bacon and cook. Add green peppers, tomatoes, salt and
sugar and continue cooking for a further 7 minutes. Pour
mixture into a shallow $1\frac{1}{2}$ pint sized oven dish. Separate
the eggs. Make 4 small wells in green pepper mixture and drop
2 egg yolks in each. Whisk 4 of the whites until stiff and
lightly fold in the grated cheese. Pile round the yolks.
Bake 355 deg.F. (gas No.4.) for 10 or 15 minutes.
This can be served in individual ovenproof dishes with one
egg yolk per person if desired. Green pepper base can be made
well in advance and will warm through while the eggs are
cooking in the final stage.

Mrs. Walter Smart

MRS. GIBSON'S EGG DISH

Medium-sized baking dish, served in
the same.

10 hard-boiled eggs.

15 Spring onions fried in butter.

Butter.

Breadcrumbs.

Thin cream.

Salt and pepper.

Butter baking dish.   Separate
egg whites and yolks.

A layer of breadcrumbs.

A layer of egg whites.

A layer of egg yolks.

Onions, butter, salt and pepper
until the dish is full.

Add enough cream to fill the dish.

Bake in moderate oven until done
and brown.

Mrs. N. Lancaster.

FRIZZLED EGGS

One egg per person.

A good tomato sugo* - best bought in tins - loosened
and heated up with a little stock - is served as a
sauce with this dish.

Have a pan of smoking hot oil ready.   Break each
egg carefully into a cup or ladle and gently stir
up the white without breaking yolk.   Season.   Tip
into fat and stand aside quickly as you may get
burnt.   The egg will frizzle up into a sort of
brown bird's nest and you must then fish it out
with a wire chip ladle and drain it on greaseproof paper while you cook the others.   The yolk
should be quite soft inside.   Sprinkle with fried
parsley and serve piled high on silver dish.   Hand
the hot tomato sugo with it.

*   The tinned tomato sauce that Italian's make
    much better than us and that can be bought in
    tubes or cans from any good grocer.

(From the late Lady Charles's Turkish Cook
  at the British Embassy, Istanbul)

EGGS STEINBECK   for 4 people

Sliced hard-boiled eggs (4 or 5)
Chopped green bacon - or ordinary bacon and a little smoked
                                    or garlic sausage
Grated cheese   -   butter   -   breadcrumbs

Slice 4 or 5 hard-boiled eggs and put them in a greased pie
dish, in alternate layers with raw, thickly chopped bacon.
Green bacon is best, or ordinary bacon with a little garlic
or smoked sausage added, according to taste.   Finish with
an egg layer and cover with grated cheese and a few crumbs
of butter and breadcrumbs made from dry bread.   Bake in
a moderate oven for 10 - 15 minutes.

EGG AND MUSHROOM   for 6 people

6 eggs $\frac{1}{2}$ lb. mushrooms
1 tablespoonful cream   6 potatoes

Simmer $\frac{1}{2}$ lb. mushrooms in milk and butter and when tender
chop very finely.   Scramble six eggs lightly using only butter
and a tablespoonful of cream.   Add mushrooms and fill 6
scooped out baked potatoes with mixture.   Pipe the edge round
with pureed potato and brown a little under a grill.

MRS. GRADY'S EGG DISH   for 6 people

6 eggs	2 medium onions
6 tablespoonfuls cream	5 tomatoes

Cut two medium onions into rings, sweat in butter till golden brown, and turn into bottom of flat fireproof dish that has been greased.   Season with salt and pepper, cover with a layer of sliced and skinned tomatoes. Season again, and break in eggs carefully.   Cover with about 6 tablespoonfuls of cream.   Add a little black pepper and bake in a hot oven until the eggs are just set, but not too firmly, - about 15 minutes.

EGGS IN BLACK BUTTER   for 4 people

2 tablespoonfuls butter	1 tablespoonful Worcester
4 eggs	sauce
chopped parsley	4 rounds of thinly sliced bread

Melt the butter in small frying pan or omelette pan and heat until it burns and goes black.   Put in Worcester Sauce and a squeeze of lemon juice.   Fry eggs very gently in this sauce, basting well. When set, trim into rounds with pastry cutter. Drain.   Fry bread in sauce and serve with eggs on top of fried bread.   Decorate with pinch of finely chopped parsley. Pour rest of sauce round eggs.   Some people like a little cream added to sauce at the end.

Hole of Ellel, Cark-in-Cartmel,
Lancashire.

EGG CASSEROLE À LA MADRAS   for 4 people

4 hard-boiled eggs chopped   1 dessertspoonful curry powder
  coarsely   4 tablespoonfuls chicken stock
2 large onions cut in small   1 tablespoonful chutney funghi
  pieces and fired with garlic   or mushrooms chopped if
¼ pint of cream   desired
brown breadcrumbs   salt
                                  pepper

Simmer everything (except eggs, cream breadcrumbs) for half-
an-hour.   Add eggs, cream, breadcrumbs.   Mix and put in
a greased gratin dish and bake in a moderate oven for half-
an-hour.

The Hon. Mrs. Ian Campbell Gray.

OEUFS MOLLETS en SOUFFLÉ

6 Eggs
½ pint Béchamel Sauce made of
1 oz butter
1 oz flour
½ pint milk
2 oz grated Parmesan cheese
Pepper and salt.

Boil four eggs by adding them to water already
boiling, from four to five minutes. Plunge
in cold water or put in frigidaire for eight
minutes. Peel. Make Béchamel sauce, adding
cheese away from fire but when sauce is hot.
Cool and add 2 egg yolks to sauce. Beat two
remaining whites of eggs very stiffly and fold
into sauce. Put a little of this mixture into
bottom of dish. Add the four peeled eggs and
fill up the dish with the rest of the sauce.
Bake for 15-20 minutes. Gas oven heat 6.
The eggs should still be just soft inside when
the dish is ready.

Lady McEwen

WHITING AND TOMATO SOUFFLÉ

(frequently mistaken for Salmon)

Ingredients

    3 medium sized whiting skinned & curled
    ¼ pint water
    ¼ pint milk
    3 oz. butter
    2 oz. flour
    3 teaspoonfuls of tomato purée
    4 eggs
    salt and black pepper

Steam the whiting in the water with a pinch of salt
for 20 minutes.   Keep liquid on one side.   When
fish is cold remove all bones carefully.   Melt
butter in a saucepan.   Stir in flour and add the
milk and the liquid in which fish was cooked.
Season with a little salt & black pepper.   Stir
until it thickens, then add tomato purée, whiting
and the yolks of the eggs.   Lastly whip the whites
of egg until stiff & fold into the mixture.   Turn
into soufflé dish.   Bake in hot oven for 20 minutes.

Lady Douglas-Home.

Strachur House,
Argyll.
Tel. Strachur 242.

MEXICAN RISOTTO   for 6 - 8 people

1½ tumblers of rice   6 eggs
6 bananas   4 rashers bacon
1 small onion   almonds

                        sultanas

This is a risotto made in the usual way of cooking 1½ tumblers
of rice for 12½ - 14 minutes*   in salted boiling water, washing
it under cold water in a collander or tambour sieve and drying
it in a low oven for about 1 hour. When dry turn into large
frying pan in which you have been sweating one small finely
chopped onion in butter - or oil.   Add to this, 6 hard-boiled
eggs quartered, 6 small bananas (ladies fingers), slightly
over-ripe if possible, split in half, a handful of sultanas, and
peeled almonds and a little chopped crisply grilled bacon.

* Take a spoonful out after 12½ minutes, wash in cold water
  and test. It should not be too soft.   The time variation
  depends on what type of rice is used, Patna, Italian or
  American.

MUSHROOMS AND FROMAGE

1 lb. Button Mushrooms (tinned do quite well).
3 Tablespoonfuls thick Cream.
4 Dessertspoonfuls grated Gruyere Cheese.
4 ozs. Butter.

Peel mushrooms and cook in butter.
Add cream, heat thoroughly then add
Gruyere cheese.   Put in gratin dish and
sprinkle Gruyere cheese on top.   Brown
under grill.   Serve immediately.

————

4 persons.

Mrs. Stirling of Keir
(Mrs. Alice Thomson)

BEAUFORT CASTLE,
BEAULY,
INVERNESS-SHIRE.

OEUFS SAVOYARDE

Take a fireproof dish, rub it with garlic and butter it well. Parboil, in their skins, one pound of floury potatoes, peel them & cut them in thin slices. Dispose of these in layers in the fireproof dish, sprinkling salt & pepper on each layer. Put in a little cream, just level with the potatoes, and put the whole thing in a moderate oven (Regulo 6) Cook it till the potatoes are quite soft and the cream ~~reached~~ reduced.

Meanwhile, poach 4 eggs in boiling salted water (with very little vinegar in it.) Five minutes will do, as the yolk should remain liquid. Remove & drain them well; dispose them on the top of the potatoes; sprinkle a little grated cheese (Parmesan & Gruyère mixed in equal parts), & glaze quickly under the grill.

Lady Lovat
(Miss Dorothy Fraser).

TELEPHONE BEAULY 206.
STATION INVERNESS.

BEAUFORT CASTLE,

BEAULY,

INVERNESS-SHIRE.

OEUFS HOMEFIELD

1 can tomatoes
   chopped parsley
4 large onions,
   pepper, salt, french mustard.

Chop onions finely and fry till tender, add

tomatoes, chopped parsley, seasoning,

1 teaspoon french mustard and cook for 10

minutes, take off heat and add 2 yolks of eggs,

and 2 tablespoons cream, do not cook again just

keep hot.

Poach the number of eggs required and put on

croutons of fried bread, spoon the sauce over

the eggs and serve.

Lady Lovat
(Miss Dorothy Fraser).

GREEN OMELETTE   for 6 people

Spinach purée   7 eggs
1 large carton Morecambe shrimps   Butter
              Olive Oil

This is a soufflé omelette, made in the usual
way, that is, you beat half the whites of egg
to a stiff froth separately and fold into the egg
mixture just before pouring into a smoking hot
omelette pan.   I always use half butter and half
olive oil in my pan to get it really hot without
burning.   The green colouring is made by adding a
dessertspoonful of spinach purée (frozen spinach
purée will do, but cook out the water) into the egg
mixture before folding in the egg whites.   The
shrimps have been heating in another pan and you
fill the omelette with these and fold over.   Put
into a very hot oven for two or three minutes and
it will rise a bit.   Serve immediately.

Lady Peake
(Tonshika)

Bruern
Churchill
Oxford

PÂTES VERTES   Serves 6.

8 oz. Spinach Spaghetti
3 tomatoes peeled & emptied
4 large mushrooms
2 small onions sliced & blanched
3 slices ham
1 red pepper, peeled and diced (or tinned)
  garlic to taste
  grated gruyere for top
1½ pints rather thin white sauce
  salt and pepper

Cook spaghetti in boiling salted water from 10-12
mins.   It should not be too soft.   Dice ham, slice
mushrooms and sauté in oil.   Drain spaghetti.   When
cooked in a large bowl mix together all ingredients
and check seasoning.   Pour into a buttered oven
dish, top with grated cheese and brown in a hot oven.

The Hon. Mrs. Michael Astor

Strachur House,
Argyll.
Tel. Strachur 242.

"SUGO" for Spaghetti Bolognese

Boil the spaghetti in boiling salted water for
12-14 minutes - (leave it long - half the fun is
watching other people eat it) strain - add a large
nob of butter, grated parmesan cheese and spoon on
to each helping the following Bolognese sauce or
sugo - a <u>large</u> spoonful of it.

The Sugo -

One large onion finely chopped fried in 1 tablespoonful butter and 1 tablespoonful of oil.   Add
2 heaped tablespoonfuls finely chopped cooked meat
- (beef or veal or pork) a tablespoonful of Italian
tomato puree (tin or tube) and a tablespoonful
Heinz Tomato sauce and a bayleaf.   Simmer all
together, season well - remove bayleaf before serving.   Enough for 4-6 people.

from my Yugo Slav kitchen

61 EATON TERRACE

S.W. I

SLOANE 5782

Spinach Roll   (for 6 people)

Boil 2 lbs of spinach, drain
thoroughly, then cut it up very finely
with a knife (this could be done
in a Mix-Master)
Make a thick Béchamel sauce &
add it to the Spinach. 3 yolks of eggs
Salt, pepper, a pinch of nutmeg & 2-3 tbs
of grated cheese. Whisk the whites & fold
in to the mixture.   Grease a baking tin
sprinkle it with flour & put in a layer of
spinach (1 finger thick) - bake for 10 minutes
in a hot oven.   Before serving cover the
spinach with Sauce Béchamel, then roll it
(like a Swiss roll) - Some more sauce could
be added when rolled.

Lady Peake
(Tonshika)

—45—

Swiss Eggs.

6. eggs.
6. thin slices of Gruyère cheese.
1/4. pint single cream.
salt and black pepper.
Butter . . . . (serves 6,)

Butter a long fireproof dish, cover the bottom of the dish with the slices of cheese. Break the eggs on top and cover with the cream. Season well, and cover with shavings of butter. Bake in a moderate oven, until the whites are set, but the yolks should be fairly runny. Serve hot.

Mrs. Richard St. Clair
de la Mare.

Mrs. Richard St. Clair de la Mare.

TOMATO AND CAULIFLOWER AU GRATIN   for 6 people

1 cauliflower	3 ozs grated cheese
5 tomatoes	2 eggs
¾ pint béchamel sauce	butter

1 tablespoonful cream

Part cook one large cauliflower in salted water. Break up
into pieces and put into greased, not too shallow entree dish.
Skin 5 tomatoes by pouring boiling water over them and slice.
Add to cauliflower and season well. Make ¾ pint of white
sauce. Season well. Add 2 ozs grated cheese, and a
tablespoonful of cream. Separate two eggs, add yolks to
sauce and beat whites very stiffly. Take sauce from fire
and cool a little. Fold in whites and pour over cauliflower
and tomato. Sprinkle top with crumbs of butter and grated
cheese. Put into a hot oven for 15 - 20 minutes till well
risen.

LIVER KREMOSKIES

¼ lb. Puff Pastry (the Lyons bought
          kind is excellent).
3 or 4 Chicken Livers.
Chopped Onion.
3 slices of Bacon.
Pepper and Salt.
Butter for frying.
Oil for deep frying.
1 tablespoonful of Meat Gravy.
1 Beaten Egg.
A little Vermicelli.

Cut the livers in slices and saute very fast in hot
butter.   Chop finely and add already fried chopped
onion and bacon.   Mix and season well, and add one
tablespoonful of brown gravy.

Roll out pastry to florin thickness.   Cut into
rounds the size of a small teacup top.   Put a
teaspoonful of the filling in the middle of each
round, brush edges with beaten yolk of egg and fold
over.   Roll in beaten egg and raw vermicelli, and
fry in very hot deep fat or frying oil until golden
brown.   A good meat gravy can be served with them
or sauce espagnole.

GNOCCHI CON FORMAGGIO

$\frac{1}{2}$ pint milk   6 eggs
$\frac{1}{2}$ lb flour $\frac{1}{4}$ lb grated cheese (cheddar will do)
$\frac{1}{4}$ lb butter   salt, pepper.

Simmer the milk and butter in a saucepan and sift in the flour gradually, beating well with a wooden spoon. Add the eggs, one by one; take off the fire for a really good beat whenever you are frightened of it "catching"; then lastly add the cheese and cook for another few minutes — (just as for "choux paste.")

Put the paste into a forcing bag with a plain one inch nozzle and squeeze it out, cutting off pieces like thick pennies into a saucepan of boiling water. Poach for ten minutes (they should then be the size of marshmallows), drain and lay in a flat fireproof entree dish; cover with white sauce to which $\frac{1}{2}$ a cup of cream has been added and sprinkle the top with grated cheese. Put into a medium oven for 20-25 minutes and serve very hot and slightly browned on top.

Lady Jekyll

A little practice is needed for making the paste which is a cheesy choux paste (as used for eclairs and beignets); but energetic beating is the main answer.

IMAM BAILDI   (Father Fainted)

2 Aubergines.
4 tablespoonfuls Salad Oil.
1 oz. Butter.
4 medium sized Onions.
4 large ripe Tomatoes, peeled and emptied
                                    of pips.
2 finely chopped Sweet Peppers.
1 teaspoonful chopped Parsley.
1 teaspoonful chopped Thyme.
Grated Cheese - Parmesan or Cheddar.
Brown Crumbs.
Seasoning.
Melted Butter.

Cut the Aubergines in half and with a knife slit round
the edge and several times across.   Sprinkle with salt
and leave for 30 minutes.   Drain, dry and place them
face down in a frying pan which holds the heated oil.
Fry 7 minutes turning them once or twice and adding
more oil if necessary.   Lift out when brown and scrape
the meat carefully from the skins, chop coarsely. Melt
the butter in a pan, add onions, cook slowly without
colouring, add the tomatoes, sweet peppers, aubergine
meats, herbs and seasoning, simmer for 5 minutes.
Fill the mixture into the skins, dust well with cheese
and breadcrumbs, sprinkle melted butter over each and
finish under the grill or in the top of hot oven.

These are also delicious eaten cold, slightly chilled.

The name derives from the Turkish tale that when the
Imam in question was first presented with this delicacy,
he swooned from sheer delight.

RISOTTO ALLA MILANESE

2 ozs. Butter.
1 medium sized Onion, chopped finely.
1 oz. Beef Marrow - (optional).
12 ozs. Italian rice.
4 tablespoonfuls dry White Wine.
About two pints hot Chicken Stock.
Grated Parmesan Cheese.
A pinch of Saffron.
Salt and Pepper.

Melt 1 oz. of Butter in a saucepan and over low heat
fry the onion until soft and golden.   Stir in the
beef marrow if used.   Add the rice and stir until
translucent, then add the wine and cook until almost
evaporated.   Add the hot stock in three or four
instalments, cooking over moderate heat, without
a lid and stirring from time to time.   Towards
the end stir continuously to avoid sticking.   It
should take from 25 to 30 minutes.   Finally add
the saffron previously dissolved in a little stock,
the remaining butter, a heaped tablespoon of cheese,
and salt and pepper to taste.   Serve the risotto with
more Parmesan handed separately.

This kind of risotto is meant to be sticky, the
grains are bound together by the sauce and are not
separate and dry as in curry rice.

It makes a nice luncheon dish if the rice is put
into an oiled "baba" mould for the last 5 - 10
minutes and finished off in the oven.   When the
mould is turned out, fill the centre with stewed
mushrooms that have been tossed in cream.   Serve
grated Parmesan separately.

Cold First Course
or Supper Dishes.

CHICKEN LIVER PATÉ.

2. Onions
½ lb. Bacon from which the fat should be trimmed off.
2. Cloves of Garlic
25. Chicken Livers
1½ Pints of Double Cream

Chop finely the onions and the bacon and fry them in oil and butter until brown. Pass through the liquidiser with the livers and a little pepper and salt. Pass through wire sieve, add the cream, mix all together and put in shallow Pyrex dish. Stand in water and cook slowly for 2½ to 3 hours. When cold, put in dish or bowl and cover with melted butter or margarine. The quantities here given will make enough paté for about 30 people, or may be used for smaller numbers on several separate occasions. Replaced in the fridge each time after use, it will keep a month if well sealed with butter. It should be eaten on crisp toast and served in the same way as "paté de foie gras".

The Lady Egremont

Hole of Ellel, Cark-in-Cartmel,
Lancashire.

COLD CHEESE SOUFFLÉ   for 4 people

2 ozs. finely grated Parmesan   Nearly ½ pint of cream
2 eggs   salt
              cayenne pepper

   Separate the yolks from the whites.   Beat yolks
to a cream, add the cheese, seasoning, then the cream
medium whipped, then the whites stiffly whipped.
Place low in the icebox, all day if possible.

The Hon. Mrs. Ian Campbell-Gray.

SMOKED SALMON MOUSSE

One large cup of chopped smoked salmon which should
be reduced to a fine puree in electric mixer (or
rubbed through a fine wire sieve), add to this
½ teaspoon lemon juice, ¼ teaspoon paprika, then
lightly add in a cup of ½ whipped cream; when all
is mixed add three tablespoons liquid aspic jelly;
pour into souffle dish, sprinkle on top a thin
layer of caviar; set in refrigerator, and when
set put a thin layer of aspic on top.

*   *   *

SMOKED HADDOCK MOUSSE   (for 6)

1 lb. Smoked Haddock on the bone or
¾ Smoked fillet.
2 eggs, hard boiled
cold Bechamel sauce made with
¼ oz. butter, ¼ oz. flour, ½ pint milk, ¼ pt. Mayonnaise,
½ oz. gelatine, ½ gill light stock or water, ½ gill cream.
To finish 2 hard-boiled eggs,
1 pint Aspic jelly.

Have ready the fish, cooked, skinned and flaked, and
the eggs chopped. Mix the sauce and mayonnaise
together. Dissolve the gelatine in the stock over
a gentle heat and add to the sauce with the fish and
eggs. Lightly whip the cream and fold into the
mixture. Turn onto a souffle dish three parts
full and leave to set. Decorate the top with
sliced hard boiled egg and spoon over enough cold
aspic to hold them in position. Leave to set and
then fill the dish with more aspic.

Mrs. V.F. Cavendish Bentinck.

Bruern
Churchill
Oxford

Melon a l'Anis

2 small ripe melons
2 teaspoons of anis liqueur
4 teaspoons of powdered sugar
8 teaspoons of water

Cut the melons in half, remove the seeds with a spoon.
Mix anis, sugar & water together in a glass untill the sugar has melted.
Sprinkle this mixture over the melons and keep them in a cool place untill ready to serve.

Serves 4.

The Hon. Mrs. Michael Astor.

COLD CRAB SOUFFLÉ

For 6 to 8 people.

Take a crab weighing about $3\frac{1}{2}$ lb. Remove all fish from
the shell and one claw; put into a basin, season with
salt and pepper, add a teacupful of mayonnaise sauce and
one of liquid aspic jelly. Mix all well together, and
stir in 4 leaves of dissolved gelatine. Lay at the bottom
of a fluted white china or silver souffle dish some lettuce
leaves, shredded, and some slices of tomato; half fill
with the prepared crab, then cover with part of the meat
flaked from the other claw, cover with the rest of the
mixture, then the rest of the claw. Leave this to set.
Before serving it very cold cover the top of the souffle
with finely-chopped aspic jelly, and send round sandwiches
of brown or white bread with green filling.

Lady Jekyll.

4 leaves of gelatine equal just over $\frac{1}{2}$ oz. of the powdered kind.

This is a much nicer starter to a dinner party than the
useful but ubiquitous crab/lobster cocktail with its techni-
colour pink sauce, – and no more trouble, especially if you
buy the aspic jelly (or jellied consommé) in a tin or a
bottle from a good grocer.

VENISON PÂTÉ

About ¾ lb. Venison, any part, but trimmed carefully of gristle and sinews.

¼ lb. Bacon.

Cook Venison lightly in butter, mince with Bacon
and any juice or butter there is from the cooking.

Make a sauce with just over 1 oz. of butter, just
under 1 oz. of flour, and about ½ pint of milk,
infused with onion, bayleaf, and pepper corns.

Pound the meat, add about 2 teaspoonfuls Tomato
puree (preferably strong Italian), and clove of
Garlic squeezed. Add the sauce and salt and mix
well.

Put in greased tureen or any suitable dish.

Stand in bain-mari in oven for short while. (Not
essential).

Serve buttered toast.

Mrs. John Noble.

SLEDMERE
DRIFFIELD
YORKSHIRE.

PHEASANT PÂTÉ

Take a brace of pheasants and cut all meat
off bones. Cover bones with water and simmer
for two hours, then add one ounce of gelatine to
the liquid. Mince the pheasant meat together
with a half pound of bacon, add liquid, put in a
baking dish and cover with strips of bacon.
Bake for 1½ - 2 hours at about 400°F. When
cold remove bacon strips and cover pâté with
melted butter. Will serve eight over a week-end.

Lady Sykes
(Mrs. Scott)

STUFFED GREEN PEPPERS

1 teaspoonful curry powder	6 hard-boiled eggs
½ pint cream	4 tablespoonfuls chopped ham
6 green peppers	¼ small cucumber, diced

Cut off tops and take out seeds of 6 medium-sized green peppers.
Blanch by throwing them into boiling salted water for five or
six minutes. Drain.   Fill with a mixture of a creamy white
sauce (use half cream, half milk), mixed with a teaspoonful of
curry powder, chopped ham, cucumber and hard-boiled eggs.
Serve very cold.

SALADE NICOISE

There are many versions of this dish but the most important
ingredient is a very large wooden bowl. The rest is up to
individual taste.   I put -

3 or 4 lettuces	¼ pint of black olives
5 tomatoes quartered	1 small tin of anchovies
1 tin of sardines	six hard-boiled eggs, quartered
a little diced cucumber and a few radishes	

into mine - and I make a 'French' dressing of -

6 tablespoonfuls olive oil	a clove of crushed garlic
1½ tablespoonfuls French	(optional)
wine vinegar	1 teaspoonful salt
some French mustard	1 teaspoonful pepper
more black pepper if necessary	

Chopped tarragon is nice thrown over salad when mixed. It must
be well mixed and kept very cool. It is a delicious first course
for a hot day.

Strachur House,
Argyll.
Tel. Strachur 242.

MOUSSE OF TUNNY FISH

$\frac{1}{2}$ lb. cooked Tunny Fish
freed from skin and bone
$\frac{1}{2}$ pint cold Béchamel sauce,
made with $\frac{3}{4}$ oz. butter
$\frac{3}{4}$ oz. flour and
$\frac{1}{2}$ pint flavoured milk
1 whipped egg white

$\frac{1}{4}$ pint mayonnaise
scant $\frac{1}{2}$ oz. gelatine dissolved
in 2 - 3 tablespoonfuls light
stock or water
2 - 3 tablespoonfuls partially
whipped cream
2 ozs. prawns or shrimps

Garnish: Watercress; hard-boiled eggs; mayonnaise
to coat; extra prawns if wished; black olives

Pound or work the tunny fish until smooth, add by degrees the
Béchamel sauce and mayonnaise. Season, fold in dissolved
gelatine, cream, coarsely chopped prawns and lastly egg
white.   Turn at once into a lightly oiled mould and leave to
set. Turn out, coat with mayonnaise lightened with a little
tomato juice and seasoned with Tabasco. Garnish with sieved
yolk and shredded hard-boiled egg white and 'bouquets of
watercress' and black olives.

Strachur House,
Argyll.
Tel. Strachur 242.

IVAR

4 aubergines
1 large clove of garlic
crushed to a cream with salt
1 shallot chopped very fine
2 small green peppers, as hot
as possible (they should smell
peppery) chopped very fine

salt
freshly ground pepper
a dash of cayenne
lemon juice
olive oil to taste:
about a cupful

Wrap each aubergine in oiled paper, set on a tin and bake
in a moderate oven until soft - about 40 minutes. Cool,
split, and scrape the pulp out carefully with a silver
spoon. Chop slightly and turn into a bowl. Add other
ingredients and mix.* Season well and sharpen with lemon
juice. Eat iced very cold as a side salad to a main meat
course, or as hors d'oeuvre, in which case warm oatcakes
and fresh butter are good served with it.

* The olive oil should be beaten in slowly, a teaspoon at
  a time.

Hors d'oeuvres

Any two, three, or more of these dishes, if prepared with loving care, are good starters for a summer meal.

STUFFED HARD BOILED EGGS

Halve eggs when cooked and shelled, take out yolks and mix with any of the following:

Curry powder and cream
Tomato sugo and a little mayonnaise
Chopped fried bacon and onion and a drop of
                                    worcester sauce
Shrimps pounded with a little cream cheese and a
                                    spoonful of cream
Tunny fish, mayonnaise, black pepper and lemon juice.

When smoothly blended, pipe back into halved whites.

WHITE BEANS AND TUNNY FISH

One can Butter Beans or cold cooked Haricot Beans.
One small tin of Tunny.
Olive oil, pepper freshly ground, salt, a little raw chopped onion, garlic if wished, lemon juice.

Mix together and marinade for a few hours in a cold place.

GREEN PEPPERS PIEDMONTESE

De-seed peppers. Stuff them with quartered, seeded tomatoes some anchovy fillets that have been pounded with garlic and mixed with olive oil. Bake for 30 minutes in moderate oven and eat cold.

CHICKEN LIVERS

Chop finely, saute in butter and a little chopped onion.
Pile on buttered toast fingers.

RAW MUSHROOMS

Remove stalks and wipe about 15 mushrooms (average size,
button shape) carefully with damp cloth.   Cut in very
thin slices vertically - keeping mushroom shape.   Pour
over a marinade of 4 tablespoonfuls olive oil mixed with
the juice of two lemons and a little finely chopped
parsley and leave in a cold place for at least 2 hours
before serving.

CAULIFLOWER

Use only the florets of one large cauliflower boiled in
salted water, drained, chilled and covered with a good
lemon mayonnaise (use lemon juice instead of vinegar)

If you like raw vegetables, these are also delicious uncooked, with the mayonnaise in a bowl to be dipped into.

ANCHOVY FILLETS

In oil - arranged in a flat dish, or, for a buffet party,
on a huge block of ice.

SKINNED TOMATOES

Marinaded in oil and vinegar and sprinkled with chopped
Dill.

SMOKED DALMATIAN or AUSTRIAN HAM

This can be bought in sausage shape and is less expensive
than real Parma ham.   It need only be cut into very thin
slices, and like Parma ham can be eaten with Melon or Green
Figs.

HOME MADE SMOKED SALMON

See p. 108   recipe for DILLED SALMON.

SMOKED EEL

Can be bought at any delicatessen.   Trim and cut into
2 inch strips.   Serve with Rye bread or Wholemeal bread.

The Corner House,
62, Wellington Road, N.W.8.

HORS D'OEUVRES

Cold sweet corn.

2 tins   Whole Kernel corn.
Strain off liquid through seive.
Salt and Pepper according to taste.

Dessertspoonful of sifted white sugar, or as much as desired.

Stir the whole together in slightly whipped double cream.

Place in refrigerator.

Take two hard-boiled eggs, cut them in thin slices and garnish

the top of the cold cream corn.

Make a mayonnaise with cream added to it but keep it as thick

as possible and pour it over the top of the corn and hard-boiled

eggs.   A little curry powder can be added to this.

Devilled Sardines

1 or 2 tins Sardines according to the necessity.

After removing middle bones and tails, mash them with a fork.

Put a dessertspoonful of Worcester Sauce, or more according to

taste into the mixture.

Two teaspoonfuls of honey

Two good teaspoonfuls of unmade mustard

A dessertspoonful of Harvey Sauce if you have got it, or

Sauce Robert.

Salt and Pepper.

Add two tablespoonfuls or more of Tomato Ketchup, mash this

mixture fairly fine and serve.

It can be made hot on hot buttered toast.

Rhoda, Lady Birley

NOTES

NOTES

Poultry & Game.

CORTACHY CASTLE
KIRRIEMUIR
ANGUS

DEVILLED GROUSE   for 6 people

3 grouse
½ pint cream
1 bay leaf
Worcester Sauce
Sauce Diable

3 ozs. Patna rice
2 ozs. sultanas
Curry powder
1 tin Campbell's Consommé
Bovril

Dress grouse as for roasting and put in oven covered by good dripping and tinfoil, 30 minutes being quite sufficient in hot oven. Put rice in small pan and cover with consommé. Add bay leaf plus one teaspoonful curry powder and sultanas. Allow to simmer very slowly until rice is cooked and nearly dry. Avoid stirring as rice will become gluey. Remove grouse from oven and cut each bird cleanly in half. Place in serving dish and allow to cool then cover with whipped cream to which has been added 2 teaspoonfuls Worcester sauce, 1 teaspoonful Bovril and 2 tablespoonfuls Sauce Diable. Place cooked rice round about bird halves and put back in hot oven for 10 minutes to heat through and serve at once with usual vegetables and game crisps.

Lady Ogilvy
(Mrs. Chrissie Hanton)

PORTSONACHAN,

BY DALMALLY,

ARGYLL.

GROUSE SALAD

This is a delicious way of serving cold grouse.

2 cold Grouse.
2 finely chopped Shallots.
3 dessertspoonfuls Tarragon and Chervil mixed.
4 dessertspoonfuls Castor Sugar.
2 yolks Eggs.
Salt, Pepper and little Cayenne.
6 tablespoonfuls Salad Oil.
4 dessertspoonfuls Tarragon Vinegar.
1 gill whipped Cream.
2 hard-boiled Eggs.
2 Beetroot.
Anchovy fillets.

Carve the cold grouse into thin slices taking all off the bone.   Surround with diced beetroot, hard-boiled egg and anchovy fillets.   Pour over a dressing made as follows:-

Mix the shallots with the herbs, add the beaten egg yolk and the castor sugar, pepper, salt and cayenne.   Now stir in the salad oil and the vinegar and finally the whipped cream.   Sprinkle with chopped parsley before serving.

Mrs. James Young

GAME PIE

2 lb. Calf's Liver, 2 lb. not very fat Bacon, cut into
squares, a walnut piece of Butter, Pepper, Salt and
Spices, Parsley and Shallot finely chopped. Fry these
gently together. When cooked, put them into a mortar,
after first removing the fat, pound well, and season
highly.

Bone and skin a Chicken, or Rabbit, or Game, cut into
moderate-sized pieces and fry in a stew-pan with butter.
Do not brown it. When cooked firm but tender, season
with allspice and black pepper.

Lay some of the pounded forcemeat at the bottom of a
large oval game pie-dish*, cover with a layer of chicken
or game, mixing the white and brown meat, and so on till
the dish is full, ending with a top layer of forcemeat.
Put this game pie-dish into a stew-pan half-full of water
on the fire for 2 or 3 hours, according to size. When
cooked press contents tightly down and round the dish
and flatten with a wooden spoon. Pour clarified butter
thinly over the top to exclude air; garnish with broken
aspic and parsley.

Lady Jekyll

* Very pretty game pie-dishes with lids that look like
  pastry croûtes can be bought from the General Trading Co.,
  in Sloane Street.

DEVILLED TURKEY

This is a good dish for using up cold chicken or turkey.
It is also an excellent main dish for a dinner party or
a buffet supper.

Roast turkey and take all white meat and good dark meat
off carcase. Lay in a shallow entrée dish.   Pour devilled
sauce over and bake in oven for 10 - 15 minutes and
garnish with fried parsley and serve.   A large dish of
plain boiled rice should be handed separately.

The Devil Sauce

$\frac{3}{4}$ cup cream ($\frac{1}{4}$ pint)
1 teaspoonful anchovy essence
1 tablespoonful Harvey sauce
1 dessertspoonful Worcester
sauce

1 dessertspoonful
mushroom ketchup
1 dessertspoonful mango
chutney
Salt, pepper, mustard,
and a dash of cayenne

Whip the cream till stiff, add the remaining ingredients
(except the chutney) by degrees, whisking gently to keep
the sauce as thick as possible.   Lastly fold in the chutney.

PHEASANT or CHICKEN SPATCHCOCK

Ordinary roast chicken or pheasant cut up and boned.
Spatchcock sauce is made of $\frac{1}{2}$ pint cream, chicken gravy
and a tablespoonful of Worcester sauce.   Put chicken in
shallow entrée dish.   Pour over sauce and serve garnished
with straw potatoes (cut into matchsticks and deep fried).

PERDREAUX à la BARETTA

12 Partridges.
 2 pts. thick Cream.
12 Green Grapes.
 6 Glace Cherries.
 1 Medium sized Apple.
 2 Small Glasses Whisky.

Put partridges in gratin dish and season.
Cover with cream.   Put in oven and cook
slowly for two hours.   After cooking one
hour add grapes and cherries and apple
cut in quarters.   Half an hour before
serving add whisky, and serve in dish
cooked in.

———

12 persons.

Mrs. Stirling of Keir
(Mrs. Alice Thomson)

Roman Pie.

Breast of Chicken (cooked)
Cooked Macaroni
Grated Cheese Sauce
Slices of ham.
Chopped onion.
Line the dish with the ingrediants
placing them in layers. When the
dish is full make a water paste.
Cover the dish with the paste. Put
it in the oven and cook for one
hour. Then let it cool, take off
the pastry and cover with aspic
jelly serve cold Season with salt
and pepper

Lady Amabel Lindsay.

RHODA'S CHICKEN PILAU *

1 boiling fowl	$\frac{1}{2}$ cup blanched almonds
2 tumblers of rice	4 or 5 hard boiled eggs
2 small onions	$\frac{3}{4}$ pint Béchamel sauce
$\frac{1}{2}$ cup sultanas	10 rashers thinly cut
	streaky bacon

Steam or boil fowl, removing giblets and livers which can
be cooked in a small saucepan. - Reserve this stock. Cook
rice in usual way and dry. Make a creamy white sauce
using half the giblet stock and half milk with a tablespoon
or two of real cream. Season well. Toss rice in a frying
pan of butter (or olive oil if preferred) and a little finely
chopped onion and bacon. Add hard-boiled eggs, sultanas
and almonds to rice and a little chicken stock, which it
will soon absorb. Lay on a large hot ashet, place cut up
and boned chicken on top and cover with white sauce. Onion
rings deep fried or sautéed till brown can serve as a garnish
round edge, and a black sliced truffle to decorate top.

Ashet is a Scottish word for large flat dish.

* Rhoda is the Mrs. Cockerill of my dedication.

Suprême Curzon

Take the skin off a 3 lb chicken,
Divide it into large pieces.
Put 2oz butter in a saucepan and
let it melt. Put 2oz of finely
chopped brunoise (celery, onion,
parsley and carrot chopped very fine)
and a sprig of tarragon. Put the
chicken in the saucepan and
cook on both sides. Add $\frac{2}{8}$ gill whisky
and cover with cream. Let it boil
for ten minutes take the chicken
out. Put 1oz butter in the sauce,
let it boil for 5 minutes. Then
pour over the chicken

Serves four people.

Lady Amabel Lindsay

6, ABERCORN PLACE,
N.W.8.
CUNNINGHAM 9021.

CASSEROLE OF CHICKEN

(4 people)

1 2½ lb chicken
4 oz butter
¼ pt cream
1 tablespoon Worcester Sauce
4 oz small mushrooms

Joint chicken carefully.   Cook gently in butter without browning.   Finish cooking in casserole in moderate oven – 45 mins.   Before serving, drain off some butter and add cream and Worcester Sauce, salt and pepper.   Return to oven for 10 minutes.   Garnish with fried mushrooms.

Mrs. Franz Osborn

Strachur House,
Argyll.
Tel. Strachur 242.

KIEVSKI KOTELET

Bone the breasts and wings of a fat young chicken,
remove skin, and any bits of muscle that look tough.
Salt. Pound slowly and carefully with wooden mallet
until quite thin. Wrap round a large nut of butter,
secure with skewer both ends. Dip in flour, then egg,
then breadcrumbs. Fry in very hot fat till golden
brown. Serve with fried parsley and allumettes
potatoes. Also serve mashed potatoes separately.

BEAUFORT CASTLE,

BEAULY,

INVERNESS-SHIRE.

COLD CHICKEN LOVAT

1 large boiling chicken with good breast.   parsley
1 pint of cream   2 onions

Boil fowl for one hour with parsley and 2 onions.
When cool, bone it and cut into pieces - not too big -
using only white meat if possible.   Put into a
greaseproof dish (Pyrex, covered) with some of the
reduced stock - a good cupful - and cook till tender,
another hour, but this depends on the toughness of the
fowl.   Pour over one pint of cream and bake for half
an hour more in moderate oven.   Leave in a cool place
till cold and then add the rest of the reduced stock
which has by now jellied into aspic and been chopped
up rather coarsely.   Sprinkle it all over top of
entrée dish which should be $2\frac{1}{2}$" high.

Lady Lovat
(Miss Dorothy Fraser)

ICED CHICKEN SOUFFLÉ WITH CURRIED LIVERS

Pound the breast of a boiled chicken, adding ½ pint
bechamel sauce, and pass it through a hair sieve, or
whirl in liquidiser. Whip ½ pint cream; add it to
the chicken. Take a white fireproof souffle dish,
stand a small jar in the centre, filling the souffle
dish around with the chicken cream. Set it in the
ice cave some 2 hours. Remove jar and fill in the
space with 6 or 8 curried chicken livers, trimmed,
and put in a stew-pan with a walnut of butter, and
seasoning. Cook these for some 10 minutes; add
1 teaspoonful each of curry powder, curry paste, and
1 tablespoonful dessicated coconut (previously steeped
and stirred in hot milk and most of the nut part
eliminated) and a little chopped shallot. Let the
livers cook in this for another 10 minutes to absorb
most of the moisture before letting them get cold
and adding to the chicken souffle. With this serve
cold curried rice and brown bread-and-butter sandwiches
with a little chutney on them.

Lady Jekyll

POULET à la CRÈME

Cut 1 or 2 small tender Chickens in half, rub them
with salt and paprika pepper. Put a good lump of
butter in small pieces into a stew-pan with some
thin slices of streaky bacon. Cover these with a
layer of onions cut into thin rings and put the pan
on the fire. When the contents begin to smoke, add
the half chickens, and let them stew on a slow fire
for 1½ hours, when they should be a light brown.
Remove from pan, carve into pieces and lay on a
hot dish. Replace stew-pan on fire, and add ½
pint sour cream, stirring constantly with a wooden
spoon. Pour this sauce upon the chickens, and serve
very hot; on no account add water or stock to this
sauce.

*   *   *

PAPRIKA STEW

Skin 4 large onions, cut up, and stew them a bright
golden colour with 6 oz. fresh butter. Rub this
through a fine sieve with ½ pint sour cream, a
saltspoonful of salt, ½ teaspoonful paprika pepper
(procurable at all stores) and add your previously
jointed and cooked chicken, or slices of cooked meat,
game, or rabbit; let this heat thoroughly and slowly;
serve in a casserole with plain boiled rice, slightly
flavoured with paprika, and a green vegetable.

Lady Jekyll

PORTSONACHAN,

By DALMALLY,

ARGYLL.

BARBECUED CHICKEN

We find this a good way of roasting chicken which
has been deep frozen, and is rather lacking in
flavour.

      1 roast Chicken.
      1 teaspoonful of any Mustard.
      1 teaspoonful of Ginger.
      1 teaspoonful salt.
      Ground Black Pepper.

Barbecue Sauce for Basting

      2 oz. Butter - melted.
      1 Onion.
      1 tablespoonful Worcester Sauce.
      H.P. Sauce.
      Tomato Sauce.
      Tomato Puree.
      1 Clove Garlic.

Chop onion finely and saute in the butter, then add
garlic, and all the liquids, and cook for half an
hour and strain. Put the chicken in a **roasting** pan,
mix the dry mustard, giner, salt and ground pepper
together and rub well into the chicken, place the
roasting pan in a hot oven and cook for twenty
minutes. Now pour over the basting sauce and
baste every quarter of an hour until cooked. Carve
the chicken, skin fat from sauce, reduce a little
and pour over the carved chicken.

Mrs. James Young.

PETTI DI POLLO ALLA BOLOGNESE

For Four.

This used to be an expensive dish and an exotic one,
but now that chicken breasts can be bought individually
in London as in Bologna we shall no doubt get used to
ordering them by the dozen.   If you have to use two
whole chickens, the wings are just as good, and the
legs will always make a casserole or rissoles for
another day.

> 4 Chicken breasts - fresh ones if you
> can get them.
>
> Seasoned Flour.
>
> 3 ozs. Butter.
>
> 4 slices of Ham, the same size as the·
> chicken.
>
> 4 tablespoons grated Parmesan cheese.
> (Freshly grated, if possible).

Remove any skin or bone from chicken breasts and flatten
with a rolling pin or meat bat.   Dip in seasoned flour.
Cook slowly (about 10 minutes) in melted butter in a
heavy frying pan over <u>gentle</u> heat.   Turn several times
until golden each side.   Lay a slice of ham on each
piece of chicken, sprinkle thickly with the grated
cheese, and spoon a little of the butter from the
pan over each.   A little white wine and/or thinly
sliced white truffles can be added at this stage if
you want the dish to be richer.   Cover the pan and
cook <u>gently</u> for another five minutes.   Arrange on a
hot serving dish and pour pan juices over.   A creamy
spinach puree is a good companion to this dish or
fresh asparagus.   A spoonful or two of cream can be
added to the pan juice at the last moment, but this
too is optional.

ROAST DUCKLING - APPLE AND RAISIN STUFFING

        2 small Ducklings.
        1 oz. Butter.
        1 Onion.
        1 lb. Apples.
        4 oz. Raisins.
        6 oz. White Breadcrumbs.
        1 Egg for binding.

Truss the ducklings for roasting and stuff with the
following:-

Melt butter, saute chopped onions and peeled, cored
and chopped apples, the raisins and finally the white
breadcrumbs, draw off to cool then add egg, blend
thoroughly.   Now roast ducklings in a hot oven
three-quarters of an hour, take out, make a good
gravy and serve accompanied by game chips and
orange and lettuce salad, with a French dressing.

Mrs. James Young.

        *   *   *

BECASSINES FLAMBÉES   (SNIPE ON FIRE)

A bird to each guest, to appear on a silver or metal
dish, perfectly roasted, and sitting each on a toast
lightly fried and spread with the liver, etc., well
pounded.   Outside the serving door let a couple of
tablespoonsful of brandy, previously warmed in a small
casserole over a spirit lamp, be set alight and poured
flaming over and around the birds just as they come to
the table.   Crisp potato straws or thin fried rounds
of Jerusalem artichoke and a salad of celery shredded
and enriched by cream, and surrounded with watercress
or lamb's lettuce, should accompany this dish.

Lady Jekyll

BEAUFORT CASTLE,
BEAULY,
SCOTLAND.

JOAN'S RABBIT SCHNITZELS

Skin and wash 2 plump rabbits.   Cut a long fillet
from either side of the back bone - flatten with
wooden mallet and shape into long thin fillets about
6" x 2½".   One rabbit should produce about 4 fillets
and the remainder can be used in a casserole.   Dust
in flour and dip in seasoned beaten egg and breadcrumbs and then fry gently in butter until golden
brown - about 8-10 minutes.

Serve in a flat dish and top each fillet with a round
slice of lemon on which you have piled, side by side,
a teaspoonful of white and yellow sieved hard-boiled
egg - pour remainder of butter around fillets and
serve accompanied by saute potatoes.

VENISON, STEWED IN RED WINE

6-8 people

Buy a piece of round, cut from the haunch, weighing about 3 lb. Put it into an earthenware or china bowl. Pour over it a coffee-cupful of olive oil (extra lubrication for the dry meat) and a third of a bottle of red wine (for flavour, and for its tenderising and preserving properties). Add a sliced onion, two teaspoons of crushed coriander seeds, herbs, ground black pepper, a clove of garlic. Cover, and leave for 24-36 hours, turning the meat now and again.

About $3\frac{1}{2}$ hours before dinner take out the meat, wipe it dry, brown it on both sides in hot meat dripping. Transfer it to a fireproof dish or casserole which has a well-fitting lid. In the same fat fry an onion, a carrot and a stick of celery, all sliced. Add these to the meat, with seasoning, pour in the heated and strained marinade. Cover the meat completely with thick slices of fat bacon, then with a double sheet of greaseproof paper, and the lid. Cook in a low oven (gas No.3, 336 deg. F.) for $3\frac{1}{2}$ hours.

To make the Sauce

Transfer the meat and bacon to a very hot serving dish, cover and leave in the oven while the sauce is sieved, and then reduced by fast boiling in a wide pan. When it begins to thicken and coat the spoon add 2 tablespoons of wine vinegar and one of sugar (I use home-made raspberry vinegar and no sugar), and as soon as it is hot again pour it over the venison, which can now be left in the oven until ready to serve.

Be sure the plates are very hot. Venison cools quicker than any other food, and the ideal is to eat it off hot-water plates. With the venison, a dish of carrots and a chestnut or brown lentil puree go admirably, but make the first and last courses very light. Venison makes most people feel particularly well fed and sleepy.

Elizabeth David

German Recipt for Hare

· Bottle white wine ·

1. Break fast cup Sour cream

2 Saddle of Hare ·

Carrots, onions, mixed herbs bay leaf ·

2 cloves. Pore fat for larding —

Marinade your hare in earthenware dish
with wine, Cut up veqtables, herbs
cloves, basting when you remember a
keeping in a cool place for 2 days.
Lard the saddles. replace in a roasting
pan. with same veqtables & liquid
adding fresh. veqtables. salt & peper.
When roasted take saddles out of
pan pour off grease. remove all
veqtables.— replace. hare in liquid.
cover with sour cream heat & serve.
Cut like saddle of Lamb —

The Countess of Hardwicke.

Fish.

SOLE au GRATIN

Butter a long fireproof dish, fillet some fair-
sized soles; chop 2 large mushrooms, a piece of
fat bacon the size of a walnut, a sprig of thyme
and parsley, and a shallot very fine; mix with
2 handfuls of fine breadcrumbs, pepper and salt,
and the juice of half a lemon.   Spread a layer
of the mixture at the bottom of the dish.   On
it place the fillets of soles, cover with the
remainder.   Place in a moderate oven for about
30 minutes, and just before serving pour a glass
of white wine over, and serve in the same dish.

Lady Jekyll

         *   *   *

OYSTERS au GRATIN

Choose the required number of plump native oysters.
Open, strain off the liquor, and beard them.   Wash
and dry the shells, butter their insides, shake over
some fine stale breadcrumbs, and replace the oyster
on a half shell.   Cover it with more breadcrumbs,
a little of its own liquor, a few grains of red or
coralline pepper, a squeeze of lemon juice, and a
very thin slice of fresh butter.   Bake 10 minutes
in a hot oven, and brown with a salamander.   Serve
hot with brown bread, butter, and a garnish of
parsley.

Lady Jekyll

73 ASHLEY GARDENS,
LONDON, S.W.1

Cold Fillets of Sole with Velouté Sauce.

Order two filleted soles with the
bones and trimmings.

Make a court bouillon with the bones
and trimmings, adding water, carrot, onion,
bouquet and cider to taste.

Cook for about an hour. Meanwhile roll
up the fillets, tie with string and put them
in a fireproof dish.

Strain the court bouillon, adding some
of it with lemon juice to the fillets.

The fillets take about twenty minutes
to cook in a moderate oven.

When cooked, strain off the liquor,
using it and the remainder of the stock as
required for the sauce. Remove string
from fillets.

Make a smooth white roux and add the
stock. When the sauce is cool, pour it
over the cooked fillets and serve cold.

From the Hon. Mrs Nigel Birch

BEAUFORT CASTLE,

BEAULY,

INVERNESS-SHIRE.

BEAUFORT SOLE WITH OYSTERS

4 Fillet Soles	2 Shallots
12 Oysters (can be tinned)	8 oz. Butter
2 Tomatoes	$\frac{1}{2}$ Lemon, parsley, thyme
$\frac{1}{2}$ Pt. White wine	

Butter a shallow earthenware dish, & spread the bottom thinly with chopped shallots, chopped thyme & parsley & juice lemon.   The sole, oysters with their juice & 2 skinned & washed tomatoes are then laid in the dish & the wine poured over.   The casserole is covered & the fish baked for about 10 mins.   The sauce is then removed from the dish & skimmed until it is reduced by half.   Next the butter is added little by little & whipped with a wire whisk.   The sauce is then poured over the sole & oysters.

Lady Lovat
(Miss Dorothy Fraser)

16 East Heath Road,
Hampstead Heath,
London.

HADDOCK à la CREME

5 fillets smoked Finnan Haddock   1 pint cream
(not frozen ones)   Black pepper

There is no finer fish in Britain than Finnan
Haddock and this is the best way of cooking it.
Insist on real smoked Finnan haddock fillets.   Throw
into boiling water for 3 or 4 minutes to remove a
little of salt.   Drain, and pick over very carefully
removing all skin, bones, and any hard pieces.   Flake
into buttered entrée dish and cover completely with one
pint of double cream.   Grate generously with black
pepper and cook in oven for about 12 minutes.   It can
be browned slightly at last moment under grill.

The Hon. Mrs. Alan Hare.

17, CHEYNE PLACE,
LONDON, S.W.3.
FLAXMAN 8824.

HADDOCK PIE   (for 6 people)

12 oz. smoked haddock, cooked, boned and skinned
 6 oz. cooked scampi
 4 oz. cooked and shelled prawns
 4 oz. cooked mushrooms
 1 pint very thick béchamel sauce
 1 glass white wine
 2 tablespoons cream
   pinch of rosemary
12 oz. puff pastry

Add the wine and the cream to the béchamel sauce, then mix in all the other ingredients. Season, if it needs it, and turn into a pie dish. Cover with the puff pastry and bake in a very hot oven for about 15 or 20 minutes.

Mrs. Richard Brooman-White.

HALIBUT STRACHUR

Fry a large piece of halibut on the bone in butter both
sides - till golden brown and till the flesh comes away
easily from the bone. Squeeze a whole lemon over fish
while frying. When ready remove fish from pan but keep
hot. Add to the sauce ½ pint cream, one tablespoonful
Worcester sauce and some more lemon juice. Correct
seasoning and pour over fish in shallow entrée dish.
Serve with straw potatoes.

HADDOCK STRACHUR

Cook haddock as on page 94 but make a creamy Béchamel
sauce to bind it with instead of pouring cream over the
fish. Roll some good puff pastry into an oblong 9" x 5"
and bake in very hot oven. When ready, split it into
two halves - fill the bottom half with the haddock
mixture and make a lid of the top half. It can be sliced
before serving.

HERRINGS IN OATMEAL

Another fish that because it is cheap is often neglected.
Herrings must be dead fresh, and it is much the best
to buy them from a small fishmonger who deals directly
with fishermen.

Split herring and flatten. Roll in coarse (pinhead) oatmeal
and fry in butter. Serve with a good creamy mustard sauce,
i.e. Béchamel, to which French mustard and a teaspoonful
of wine vinegar have been added.

SOLE AND RICE

Insist on Dover sole - in Scotland it is called Black Sole -
and have it filleted both sides. Cut fillets into 3" x 1½"
strips, roll in seasoned flour, and fry gently in butter.
Squeeze a whole lemon over fish while frying and sprinkle
with a little finely chopped parsley. Serve on bed of rice,
cooked as usual, dried, and sautéed in butter and seasoned
well with salt and black pepper.

Clouds Hill,
Offley,
Hitchin,
Offley 350.

TRUITE à la NORMANDE

4 Trout
1 Tablespoon Water
Juice of a lemon
Seasoning
Chopped Chives

Chopped Parsley
$\frac{1}{2}$ - $\frac{3}{4}$ gill cream
a few Breadcrumbs
a little melted Butter

Wash & dry trout, and lay them in a well buttered fireproof dish. Add the spoonful of water, the lemon juice, seasoning & a good scattering of parsley and chives.   Cook the trout in the oven for 10 minutes.   Meantime boil the cream for a minute or two.   Pour over the trout.   Powder with the crumbs.   Sprinkle with melted butter and brown under grill .

Lady Lloyd
(Mrs. Wright)

PRAWN OR SHRIMP CURRY

(<u>small</u> prawns or shrimps)

```
4 tablespoons of Butter.
1 large Onion, finely chopped.
Half a cup of Apple, finely chopped.
Half a cup of Celery, finely chopped.
One and a half cups of Water.
3 lbs. of Prawns or Shrimps boiled and
                              cleaned.
2 tablespoons of Curry Powder.
1 pint of Cream.
2 teaspoonsful of Liquid Honey.
Salt and Pepper to taste.
```

Put the butter in a frying pan. When melted, add the
Onion, Apple and Celery. Simmer these - then add the
water. Let all simmer gently until the apple and
celery are tender and most of the liquid has cooked
away.
Stir into the mixture the seasonings.
Add the cream and prawns or shrimps.
Cook gently until cream is reduced to a sauce.

<u>Serve</u> with rice, slightly curried with the two teaspoons-
ful of liquid honey added to it.

<u>This can also be served</u> with small bowls of Chutney,
Slithered Almonds, Pine Nuts and Pickled Peaches or
Water Melon.

Lady Birley.

♔

Inveraray Castle
Argyll.
Inveraray 2275.

GRILLED LOBSTER

This is not a dish for the squeamish to cook, but
it is ambrosia for anyone to eat.

Take as many small (about 1½ lb.) live lobsters a's
there are guests and cleave them in two with a
single blow of a butcher's chopper.   Brush them
lightly with olive oil or melted butter, sprinkle
with a pince of finely chopped herbs (basil pre-
dominating) a squeeze of lemon juice and a little
black pepper, and grill them under a hot grill
till cooked (about 7 minutes).   Serve with hot
melted butter which is also seasoned with lemon
juice and herbs handed separately.

The claws are cracked and cooked in the same
way.

The Duchess of Argyll.

LOBSTER À LA NEWBURG

1½ large cupfuls of freshly cooked lobster
    cut into small pieces
1   tablespoonful butter
¾   cup madiera or light sherry
1   cup fresh cream
    the yolks of 2 eggs
    salt, black pepper, and if possible, 1 chopped
            truffle.

Melt the butter in a heavy saucepan and put in the lobster
and the truffle, season well and cover with a lid; let it
simmer gently for five minutes. Add the wine and cook for
three minutes longer. Have ready the cream and egg yolks,
well beaten; add them to the lobster, shaking the pan well
until the mixture thickens, then serve at once.

I like this served with a border of rice, but Lady Jekyll,
who usually knows best, advises serving it "in white china
ramekin dishes, attended by gossamer slices of bread dried to
lacey crispness in a slow oven," or, less elegantly: French
toast.

Lady Jekyll.

BEAUFORT CASTLE,

BEAULY,

INVERNESS-SHIRE.

COD à la PORTUGAISE

1½ lbs. Cod.
½ pt. Tomato Sauce.
½ teaspoon chopped Parsley.
1 Onion.
1 gill White Wine.
3 ozs. Butter.
Seasoning.

Cut cod in slices ½ inch thick.   Melt Butter in saute pan.   Chop onion and fry a light colour. Put in slices of cod.   Add wine and sauce, seasoning and parsley.   Cover pan and cook gently for 5 minutes.   Take out fish and reduce sauce for 10 minutes, pour over fish and serve.

Tomato Sauce

2 lbs. Tomatoes.
2 ozs. lean Ham.
12 Peppercorns.
Mixed Herbs.
1 Onion.
1 Carrot.
Bayleaf.
Sprig Thyme.
3 oz. Butter.

Cook onion and carrot in butter, add ham, tomatoes, herbs and seasoning.   Simmer for 1 hour.   Put through hair sieve, return to saucepan and re-heat.

PAUVRE HOMME

1 lb. Potatoes.
1 large Onion.
1 lb. Cod Fillet.
4 tablespoons Milk.
2 ozs. Cheddar Cheese - grated.
Salt and Pepper.
1 Bay Leaf.

Peel and slice the potatoes about the thickness of
a florin; skin and slice the onions thinly.   Wipe
the cod, which must be dead fresh, and cut it into
small pieces.   Put a layer of cod in the bottom of
an oven-proof dish that you have previously greased
with a little butter.   Season with salt and black
pepper; cover with a layer of onion and then potato,
seasoning each layer well; continue until your dish
is full, finishing with a layer of potatoes.   Stick
in the bay leaf where it is visible for removing before you serve, add the milk, and sprinkle the top
with the grated cheese and a few crumbs of butter.

Serve with a dish of grilled or stuffed tomatoes.

SALMON QUICHE

This is an excellent way for using up left-over
Salmon.

Short Crust Pastry.
6 oz. plain flour.
A pinch of Salt.
2½ oz. Butter.
¾ oz. Lard.
Pepper.
Salt.
3½ tablespoonsful Cold Water.

Sift the flour with the salt, rub in the fat with
the fingertips, add the seasoning, mix to a firm
dough with the water.   Leave the paste in a cool
place before rolling out.

Filling:

4 oz. cooked Salmon.
2 Eggs and 1 yolk.
2 oz. grated Cheese.
Seasoning.
1 gill Cream.
½ oz. Butter.
2 oz. Onions.

Line a flan ring with the pastry.   Fill with this
mixture.   Beat the eggs and cheese together, add
seasoning and cream.   Melt the butter in a small
saucepan, add the onions thinly sliced, cook slowly
until just turning colour, add the salmon and cook
a little longer, then turn the contents of the pan
into the egg mixture, mix and pour into the pastry
case, bake in a moderate oven until a golden brown.
About 30 minutes.   Serve hot or cold.

Mrs. James Young.

BAKED SALMON

When we cook a whole Salmon, we find it retains its
flavour, and does not dry out so much if it is cooked
in the oven at a very low temperature.

1 Salmon.	Pepper corns.
1 Carrot.	Parsley.
1 Onion.	Bay leaf.

Place the Salmon in a large baking dish on 2 sheets
of greaseproof paper well greased with butter papers.
Slice the carrot and onion, arrange these on top of
the fish with the pepper corns, parsley, bay leaf,
cover with more butter papers, and wrap up in the
greaseproof paper, moisten the bottom of the dish with
water and cook for 2 to 3 hours in the bottom of the
oven at 250°.   Serve hot with Hollandaise Sauce or
cold with Mayonnaise.

Mrs. James Young.

COULIBIAC

For 10 or 12 people.

2½ lb. of Paste:

     1 lb. sieved Flour.
     6 oz. Butter.
     ½ oz. Yeast.
     ½ oz. Salt.
     4 Eggs.
     4 scant tablespoons warm Water.

With quarter of flour, the water and yeast make the
dough.   Roll it into a ball.   Keep in warm place
till double the size: Mix rest of flour with butter,
eggs and salt dissolved in few drops of water.   Work
paste, pulling it and kneading it to make it elastic.
Finally mix in the dough (or 'leaven') put into basin,
cover with cloth or blanket or newspaper will do, and
leave to ferment for 5 or 6 hours in warm place.

(You can use a choux paste instead).

Filling:

     1½ lb. Salmon cut in small slices
         (cleaned of any bones or skin, etc.)
         stiffened in butter, (or just any
         cooked salmon):

     ½ lb. Rice - cooked.
     3 Hard-boiled Eggs, white and yolks
                           dropped.
     4 oz. Mushrooms and a large Onion,
         chopped, tossed together in butter.

     1 tablespoonful chopped Parsley.

(Above according to what is available - probably more

Salmon will be needed for $2\frac{1}{2}$ lb. of the Paste).

Roll out $\frac{2}{3}$ of the paste to about 16" long and about
10" wide. Fill middle with layers of rice, salmon,
mushroom, onion and egg - finish with rice. Roll
out rest of paste, lay on top of filling. Turn up
edges, moisten and join top and bottom of 'parcel'.

Keep the Coulibiac in warm place about $\frac{1}{2}$ hour, for
paste to rise slightly.

Brush over with melted butter, sprinkle with very
fine breadcrumbs, make a slit in top. Put in
moderate oven, if possible with heat mainly from
bottom, bake 50 minutes. Remove from oven, en-
large hole, if necessary, and spoon in about 5 or
6 dessertspoonfuls of melted butter.

Mrs. John Noble.

TELEPHONE
KILCHRENAN
224.

PORTSONACHAN,
By DALMALLY,
ARGYLL.

Dill Salmon or Trout.

To each 2 lb Fish mix —

2 Tablespoons coarse Salt.

1 Tablespoon Brown Sugar.

1 Teaspoon Freshly ground Pepper

Plenty of Fresh or Dried chopped
Dill.

Clean the Fish, rinse well
cut in two lengthwise + remove
all bones. Dry well with a towel
Now put a thick layer of Dill
at the bottom of a deep container
lay oneside of the fish skin side

dish, on this, sprinkle liberally
with the mixture + plenty of dill
Cover the remaining side
in the same way, + place on
top of the 1st side skin
side up, cover with more
dill. Now place a dish on top
with weights of at least 2b
each. Leave in a cool place
a cellar, for 3 days or more.
Finally remove all liquid
+ slice + serve like smoked
Salmon

Mrs. James Young   *Phyllis Young*

NOTES

NOTES

Published by A.Hamilton Oct.r 1795.

Meat.

BEAUFORT CASTLE,
BEAULY.
INVERNESS-SHIRE.

Ox Tail

1 oxtail
2 onions
3 carrots
1 Bay leaf
Paprika pepper

peppercorns
2 oz cooking fat
1 Tablespoon flour
1 glass red wine
water to cover

Thyme, Sage, parsley

Cut the oxtail into joints & brown on all sides in the cooking fat. Add the sliced onions, flour & the wine and water. Stir in salt, pepper, bayleaf & herbs. Cook in a casserole in a slow oven for about 3 hours or until meat is tender. Add sliced carrots about ½ hour before the meat is ready.

Lady Lovat
(Miss Dorothy Fraser)

Strachur House,
Argyll.
Tel. Strachur 242.

BOEUF STROGANOV

Either raw or cooked beef fillet can be used for this
dish, cut into strips about 1 inch long by $\frac{1}{4}$" thick and
fried quickly either in butter or fat.   In another
frying pan sauté chopped onions, add to this a handful
of mushrooms and one small skinned tomato and cook
more slowly.   Combine with the meat and pour one
cupful of sour thick cream over all.   Heat through and
serve immediately.

Cream can be artificially soured by adding a dessertspoonful of vinegar or lemon juice to it one hour
previously.   This dish should always be served
accompanied by sauté potatoes.

Aiguillette de boeuf braisée

Lard a good piece of rump steak with strips of bacon fat that have been soaked in brandy. Marinate the beef for 24 hours in red wine, a small glass of brandy, sliced onions, carrots & celery, thyme, bayleaf. Remove the meat, wipe it, brown it all over in butter, put it in a saucepan, cover with the same liquid plus some veal stock, cover tightly & cook slowly in the oven for 3 or 4 hours. Remove the meat, slice it & keep it warm. Strain the liquid & remove fat, then reduce until it is a rich sauce. Pour it over the meat.

Lady Shuckburgh.

Tall Trees, Boars Hill,
Oxford.

Chicory (white Belgian)
& Ham dish.

Boil Chicory till tender
drain them; wrap a
thinly sliced piece of
Ham around each
Chicory & put side by
side into fire proof
dish.

Make a Bechamel
Sauce — add grated
Cheese — pour over
Chicory dish &
heat up in oven.

Miss Hübler.

CRAIGNISH HOUSE
LARGS AYRSHIRE
TEL. 2063

Fillet of Roast Beef.

2½ - 4 lb. fillet of Beef   Gravy
larding bacon in strips.   beef stock
¼ inch wide by 2½ inches   seasoning
long - good dripping   watercress

      Trim meat slightly - thread lardons into fillet along top of meat. Melt 3 large spoonfuls of dripping in roasting pan, put in meat and baste. Put in hot oven 450°F allowing 15 minutes to the pound. Fillet should be rather underdone.

To serve
      Pour fat from pan, add stock using ½ tea-cup, salt to taste. Heat a little whisky and pour over meat. Garnish with watercress.

Mushroom or Béarnaise Sauce
Can be handed separately

Mrs. A. D. Cameron.

see p. 224

VM.

Corned Beef Hash

1 Large tin of Corned Beef Hash -
1 Tablespoon of chopped onion .
1 Tablespoon of. Sweet Pepper (green)
1 Tablespoon . of. Butter .
½ Pint of. Sour Cream .

Sauté onions & Pepper in the butter
Add to the Corn Beef Hash .
Add Sour Cream & mix
Place all ingredients in a Casserole
dish .
Put under the Broiler till Brown.
Serve -

Can buy. This of Corn beef Hash at-
Fortnum & mason -

The Countess of Hardwicke.

MRS. BRIDGEWATER'S CASSEROLE

Shin of Beef - a cheap cut

Don't cut up beef, but remove fat and gristle. Roll
in flour and season.   Put in a large casserole with
a cup of port, a cup of stout, 2 tablespoonfuls of
mushroom ketchup, a chopped onion.

Put in oven to simmer for four hours.

Mrs. Bridgewater manages to make this casserole
delicious using only shin but I find that Scottish
shins never have enough meat on them, and have taken
to using a shoulder steak which has the same kind
of taste and is much less gristly.

PANCAKE CAKE

First prepare the Pancakes.

Ingredients:

3 Eggs.
3 well heaped dessertspoons Flour.
$\frac{3}{4}$ pint of Milk.
Season to taste.

Method:

Beat all ingredients together.   Put
$\frac{1}{2}$ teaspoon oil in hot frying pan for
each pancake.   Should make 10 or 12
Pancakes.

Cook $\frac{3}{4}$ lb. Mince Meat.

Cook enough Spinach to make $\frac{3}{4}$ lb.

Squeeze two slices of bread in milk and
mix with mince meat; also mix into mince
meat 1 or 2 egg yolks.

Place two pancakes at the bottom of your
round baking tin (preferably with removable
bottom) then a layer of mince, spinach, pancake, mince, spinach and so on until a couple
of inches below the rim.

Mix separately 2 eggs and $\frac{1}{4}$ pint of cream and
$\frac{1}{2}$ lb. of grated cheese, season with salt and
pepper and paprika, pour on top of pancake
mixture and place in moderate oven for 15 to
20 minutes.

(This can also be made with minced chicken).

The Hon. Mrs. Christopher Bridge.

Tall Trees, Boars Hill,
Oxford.

HOT POT

Put into a buttered fireproof dish

1 layer of thinly sliced potatoes
1 layer of sliced onions
1 layer of sliced carrots
1 layer thinly cut slices of meat
add salt & pepper

Continue with these layers till dish is full - potato

layer on top.   Add a cupful of water.   Put over this

tinfoil paper & lid to seal well.   Cook in oven

3 - 4 hours.

Miss Hübler

RHODA'S SHEPHERD'S PIE

2 lbs. fresh minced beef (not too fatty)

Fry in good dripping. Put into pan with two sliced
onions and simmer for 2 hours. Put into fireproof
dish. Add a good spoonful of Worcester sauce and
salt and pepper to taste. Place a layer of sliced
tomato on top, and on top of the tomatoes a layer
of potato puree (made with butter and milk).
Brown in oven, or under grill.

RHODA'S BROWN STEW

2 lbs. stewing steak.   carrots, onions.

Cut meat into pieces and roll in well-seasoned
flour (salt and pepper). Fry in good dripping
until brown all over. Put into a stewpan with
onions, also fried, and cook slowly for two or
three hours. Add carrots one hour before serving.

I have included these recipes because so few people
seem to make a really good Shepherd's Pie (Hachis
Parmcutier) or a plain brown stew.

The dripping has a lot to do with it, and the
quality of the meat, but most important of all is
the seasoning. Nothing is more delicious when it
comes off, served with a rather special green salad
and accompanied by a glass of good claret.

Sir Charles Mendl used to give a weekly luncheon
party in Paris in the '30s, to which he only asked

pretty girls and wine connoisseurs and gourmets.
The menu never varied: Haddock Souffle to begin
with and Hachi Parmentier to follow.   He regarded
these dishes as the perfect background to fine wine.

TRUFFLED LOIN OF PORK

Order as much loin of pork as you need. Get the
butcher to bone it, take off the rind and roll it
into a bolster shape. The bones and rind should
be delivered with the bolster.

Untie the pork, salt and pepper it and stuff it
with truffles and garlic. Truffles are expensive,
but a small tin is enough to inform quite a large
bit of meat. Cut the truffles lengthwise in fairly
thick slices and lay them along the meat so that
everyone has visible evidence of the presence of
the truffles. Go easy with the garlic.

Tie up again into bolster form, put the meat in a
baking tin with the bones and the rind. Brown
gently for half an hour in a moderate oven. Then
put in a pint or so of stock made with beef cube,
bouquet and a glass of white wine and the liquid,
if any, in the truffle tin.

Put the lid on the tin and cook in a low oven for
about 2½ hours. Take the meat out, let it get cold
and strain the stock into a bowl.

To serve, cut the meat downwards into fairly thin
slices and decorate with the jelly under the dripping
in the bowl.

(Incidentally, the dripping is celestial and can be
eaten on toast or used to cook potatoes).

Serve with hot boiled potatoes and a watercress
salad.

The Rt. Hon. Nigel Birch, M.P.

BAKED HAM with HONEY GLAZE

Bake a Ham in the usual way, but instead of covering
it with brown sugar, peach juice or breadcrumbs, try
a Honey Glaze.

HONEY GLAZE

      1 cup of liquid honey.
      Grated peel of half an orange.

Mix together and place on the ham 45 minutes before
removing ft from the oven.

Lady Birley.

VEAL ESCALOPES or PORK CHOPS with SHURA'S SAUCE

Veal Escalopes or Pork Chops fried in egg and breadcrumbs
with the following sauce:

SHURA'S SAUCE

    Melted butter - about a tablespoonful to each person -
containing chopped hard-boiled egg, chopped fresh fennel,
finely chopped or grated lemon rind and some capers.
    Heat and pour over crisply fried pork or veal. Garnish
with lemon slices.

Mrs. Shura Shihwarg

KIDNEYS au GRATIN for 4 people

8 Lamb Kidneys	4 Large Potatoes
2 Large Onions	Half pint Bechamel
Finely chopped parsley	with grated cheese
and Seasoning.	

Cut Kidneys (cored) into small pieces – Saute
slowly in Butter, Saute chopped onions in butter
until golden.   Part Boil potatoes and cut into
small cubes.   Add potatoes to onions and kidneys
and simmer very slowly for ½ an hour then put all
ingredients into a shallow fireproof dish, which
must be very thinly buttered and cover with bechamel and grated cheese;   leave in slow oven
until ready to serve approximately 30 minutes.

Diana Westmorland

Diana, Countess of Westmorland.

PAPRIKA GOULASH

1½ lbs. chuck or blade
bone steak
1 level tablespoonful
paprika pepper
½ lb. onions
1 tablespoonful flour
1 dessertspoonful tomato
purée
¾ - 1 pint stock

2 tablespoonfuls good dripping
or oil
2 large tomatoes, peeled,
squeezed to remove the seeds
and sliced
bouquet garni
glove garlic
1 sweet pepper

Cut the meat into large squares, brown quickly in the hot
dripping and take out. Lower the heat and put in the sliced
onions and after a few minutes add the paprika. Cook slowly
for a minute, then add the flour, purée and stock. Stir
until boiling, replace the meat, add the bouquet, crushed
garlic and seasoning. Simmer gently on the stove top or in
the oven for about 2 hours or until the meat is really tender.
Then add the pepper, shredded and blanched and the tomatoes.
Simmer for 2 to 3 minutes, then serve with a spoonful or two
of sour cream over the dish. Serve with plainly boiled nouilles
or potatoes.

The Cordon Bleu School of Cookery

PORK FILLET WITH CIDER, LENTIL PUREE

2 - 3 pork fillets
according to size
1 - 2 tablespoonfuls oil
½ oz. butter
1 small onion
1 tart cooking apple

¼ pint dry cider
about ½ - 1 gill stock
kneaded butter (butter and
flour mixed together)
1 dessertspoonful chopped
parsley

Brown the fillets all over in the oil and butter. Take out and
add the onion, finely chopped and the apple quartered, cored
and sliced. Fry for a few minutes, then replace the fillets,
add the cider and a little stock. Season, cover and simmer
25 minutes, or until tender. Take up the fillets and slice
diagonally. Keep warm, strain the gravy, return to the pan
and thicken with a little kneaded butter. Adjust seasoning,
add parsley and replace the pork. Heat gently and serve.
The dish may be garnished with rings of fried apple if wished,
and accompanied by a lentil purée into which a little chopped
raw celery has been stirred just before serving.

Lentil Purée

¾ pint Egyptian lentils
1 onion stuck with a clove
1 carrot cut in thick rounds

bouquet garni
3 - 4 tablespoonfuls good stock
2 ozs. butter

Wash the lentils very thoroughly and put to soak in tepid water,
add a little salt, the onion, carrot and herbs and bring slowly
to the boil. Simmer until the lentils can be crushed between
the fingers and thumb, then rub through a sieve. Return to
the rinsed pan and stir briskly over the heat. Add the stock
to lighten. Remove from the heat and beat in the butter and
a little pepper.

The Cordon Bleu School of Cookery.

Pork Filet.

2 filets of pork. (Chops are cheaper, but take them off the bone.)
1 large onion.
1 teaspoonful of mustard.
a sprig of rosemary.
pepper and salt.   (Serves 6.)
olive oil.   . . . . .

Slice the onion and put into a casserole (with lid.). Cut the pork into 2" cubes and put, with rosemary, mustard, and the seasoning into the casserole. Cover with the olive oil, and place in a medium oven for 1½ – 2 hrs.   Serve with baked potatoes, and a green salad.

_____

Mrs. Richard St. Clair
de la Mare.

Mrs. Richard St. Clair de la Mare.

PORTSONACHAN,

By DALMALLY,

ARGYLL.

BARBARY LAMB STEW

3 lbs. lean Lamb cut in cubes.
2 lbs. Onion sliced.
1 teaspoonful Curry Powder.
1 teaspoonful Ginger.
1 teaspoonful ground Cloves.
1 teaspoonful Nutmeg.
Mutton stock or water.
Olive Oil for frying.
½ lb. Dried Apricots soaked overnight.
Bay leaf.
Thyme.
Parsley.

We usually use the shoulder for this stew because it
is never very satisfactory when roasted owing to the
large amount of fat.

Cut the onions in thin slices. Cover the bottom of
a stew-pan with olive oil and fry the onions till soft,
then add the lamb cut in cubes and fry until the meat
is closed, now cover with hot mutton stock or water,
bring to the boil and add the spices and herbs.
Simmer for 2 hours, half an hour before serving add
the apricots. Serve with boiled rice or plain
boiled potatoes.

Mrs. James Young.

From Lady Lloyd. (Mrs Wright)

Boiled Mutton with Caper Sauce

Cut 6 lb Best neck end of
Lamb into small cutlets.
Place in pan and just
bring to the boil. Pour
off liquid and renew
water. Simmer with a
little pearl barley and
a bay leaf for 1 hour

(Cont.)

After the first half hour
add the seasoning and
6 medium sized whole
onions and some carrots,
Make a pint of Bechamel
sauce, adding a quarter
of a pint of cream and
some capers. Pour over
the meat and serve

PORTSONACHAN,
BY DALMALLY,
ARGYLL.

GIGOT OF LAMB POACHED IN MILK

Gigot of Lamb.
Milk to cover.
2 Onions.
2 Carrots.
Pepper corns.
Bouquet garni.

Remove all surplus fat from the gigot, place in a fish-kettle, pour in milk to come three-quarters of the way up the gigot, put in the onions and carrots, pepper corns, parsley thyme and bay leaf and a sprig of Rosemary.   Cover and bring gently to the boil and then simmer very gently till cooked, 2 or 3 hours according to size and age.   Now take out the gigot and keep hot.   Skim the fat from the milk in which it has been cooked and strain 2 pints.   With this make a Caper Sauce with 2 oz. butter and 2 oz. flour. Melt the butter, and stir in the flour, draw off the fire and add the flavoured milk, return to the heat and stir till boiling, then add capers.   Carve slices of the lamb on a hot ashet, cover with caper sauce and surround with carefully boiled potatoes sprinkled with parsley and young carrots cooked with sugar, and sprinkled with chopped mint.

Mrs. James Young.

Strachur House,
Argyll.
Tel. Strachur 242.

CURRY

I have eaten a lot of curries, some simple and some
so complicated that they take days to prepare - but
for my taste ordinary Mutton Curry is much the nicest
and the easiest to make.

Ideally, it should be made with fresh ingredients -
but unless you have an Indian shop nearby where you
can buy freshly ground spices, the tinned Vencatachellum
brand of curry powder is excellent.

MUTTON CURRY

As much cold Mutton as you think six hungry people
will eat, chopped into half inch cubes.

> 2 tablespoons Butter.
> 2 medium sized Onions.
> 2-3 tablespoons of Vencatachellum, or good
>   Madras curry powder bought loose from
>   an Indian grocer.
> A little dessicated coconut.
> 3 wine-glasses good stock.
> 2 tumblers Rice.

Use a heavy saucepan, **sweat** the chopped onions in 2
tablespoonfuls butter, add the curry powder, stock
and meat.   Stir and simmer very gently for at least
1½ hours.   If it gets too dry add more stock - before serving add about 1 tablespoonful dessicated
coconut - or more if it needs drying up - it should
not be too watery.   A curry depends enormously on
its presentation.   I use a **very** large flat dish,
silver or china.   In the middle I pile a mountain
of rice - and at one end I dish up the curry.   At
the other end I arrange skinned and sliced tomatoes,
sliced bananas, peeled white grapes, sultanas, hard
boiled egg in slices, raw onion rings, and fried apple
slices, all of which have been liberally sprinkled

with lemon juice.

If you have not enough room for these, they can be
arranged in a second dish. Green Mango Chutney
must be served in a sauceboat, and a very much
hotter curry sauce made from the curry powder and
stock is very popular with those who like their
curries to be breathtaking. This should be handed
separately.

RICE FOR CURRY

Proceed as for Risotto (p. 51) but when it has dried,
the rice is ready to serve. Each grain should be
separate. It can be made well in advance and kept
warm on top of stove in a sieve.

For PRAWN or SHRIMP CURRY see page 99.

PLOV FROM SAMARKAND

Put one wineglassful of oil into a cast-iron or fireproof casserole and, when it is smoking-hot, throw in a coarsely chopped onion, about 6 oz. of best end of mutton cut into cubes, and a handful of long slivers of raw carrot, cut in the shape of potato straws. Cook for ten minutes &, when ready, add three wine glasses of washed rice.

Fill up with water to 1¼" above level of meat & rice. Add salt & simmer gently (uncovered) until water is absorbed & rice cooked. (about 30 minutes). Then cover pan with a tight lid & steam for another 30 minutes. Re-season, adding more salt & pepper; mix well & serve with chives, chervil & a little raw onion to garnish.

Fitzroy Maclean.

BRITISH EMBASSY,

ISTANBUL.

BEYANDI KEBAB FROM ESKISEHIR

4 - 5 Aubergines (according to size).
1 lb. fresh Butter.
Black Pepper, Salt, Lemon Juice.
Garlic to taste.

Wrap each Aubergine in oiled paper. Set on a tin
and bake in a moderate oven for about 40 minutes.
Cool, split and scrape out the pulp with a silver
spoon and turn into a bowl. Chop slightly and
add plenty of seasoning, garlic crushed to a cream
with salt (this can be omitted) and lemon juice to
taste. Put into the mixer bowl and beat for 20
minutes adding the butter slowly. When pale green
and smooth, put in a cool place. The Kebabs, which
should be marinaded first of all in olive oil, are
grilled in the usual way on skewers, and then served
on this bed of pale green perfection. They can be
strung in a variety of ways (mutton, bayleaf, onion,
liver, kidney, tomato) according to your fancy, but
I think a plain one of mutton, bay leaf and onion, is
best; if possible cook it on a charcoal grill (there
is a good and simple Japanese one that can be bought at
Liberty's) and liberally sprinkle with lemon juice
while cooking.

OSSOBUCO FIORENTINE

One meaty knuckle of Veal sawn in 2" slices.
A little flour.
3 tablespoons Olive Oil.
2 small Carrots - sliced.
2 small Onions - sliced.
1 stick Celery - sliced.
1 Bay leaf.
6 tablespoons White Wine.
$\frac{1}{2}$ - $\frac{3}{4}$ pint Veal or Chicken Stock.
Salt and Ground Black Pepper.
1 Clove Garlic - crushed.
$\frac{1}{2}$ level teaspoon grated Lemon Rind.
1 tablespoon chopped Parsley.

Ask the butcher to cut the ossobuco from the hind
quarter of veal, sawing across the shin so that each
piece includes the bone (complete with marrow) with
a good portion of meat around it.   Coat the meat in
seasoned flour.   Heat the oil in a large and heavy
saucepan and put in the onion.   Then fry the meat
in a single layer until brown on both sides.   Remove carefully so that the marrow remains in place
and keep warm.   Add other vegetables and bay leaf
to the onions and cook over low heat for five minutes.
Add the wine and cook until almost evaporated, then add
half a pint of Veal or Chicken stock.   Bring to the
boil, reduce a little and carefully replace the ossobuco.
Cover with a tight-fitting lid and simmer gently until
tender, about 1$\frac{1}{2}$ hours.   It is fatal to let it cook too
fast.   Dish the ossobuco and keep hot.   Pass the
vegetables and gravy through a sieve to form a medium
thick sauce.   If necessary boil a few minutes to reduce.   Add the garlic (if used) lemon rind, and parsley,
and check the seasoning.   Bring to the boil and pour
over the meat.   Serve with a dish of plain boiled rice
handed separately.

It is the cooked marrow which is the bonne bouche
of every portion, and in Italy you are given special
instruments like small cheese scoops for retrieving
every succulent sliver of it.

Miss Dolly Rae

PORTSONACHAN,

BY DALMALLY,

ARGYLL.

VEAL VALENTINO

Saute some thin slices* of Veal in butter, or oil and
butter, with some sliced mushrooms for 10 minutes. Lay
them on a base of mashed potatoes. Make a roux in the
same frying pan of the butter you have cooked the veal
in, flour, and the juice from a tin of asparagus tips
and a gill of cream. Then add the asparagus tips and
pour over veal. Add grated cheese, a dash of lemon
juice and brown under grill.

*If the butcher will not cut you fine enough scallops of
veal, ask for a leg and cut them yourself from the thigh,
using a very sharp knife. Put them between greaseproof
paper and flatten with a meat bat, or if you have not got
one with the thick end of a wine bottle, which serves the
purpose admirably.

       *   *   *

ESCALOPE OF VEAL À LA CRÈME

4 slices of Veal, paper thin, butter and cream, seasoning.

We use the leg of veal for this, cutting slices from the
thigh.   Cut them as thin as possible and then put each
between greaseproof paper and flatten to paper thickness
with a batten made especially for the purpose.   Season
the slices with pepper and salt, melt the butter in a
frying pan, fry the veal gently turning once, when cooked
pour over one gill cream and allow to bubble.   Serve at
once.

Mrs. James Young

Escalope of Veal à la Marsala

Exactly the same as Veal à
la Crème except that you add
a Tablespoonful of marsala to
the cream and a few slithered
mushrooms that have been
stewed in butter — Serve
immediately.

(The undercut is the tenderest
of all, but wont feed more
than 4 or 5 people —)   V.M.

MOUSSAKA

Mince 1 lb. of Beef or Lamb very fine. (Mutton is best). Take 8 or 10 finely chopped small onions and fry them in 2 tablespoons of oil till brown. Cut 3 or 4 unpeeled Aubergines into large round slices and fry in hot oil.

Put some more oil in a deep iron casserole (about the depth of a roasting tin) and cover the bottom with aubergines; cover the aubergines with the minced meat and this with the fried onions. Season well. Repeat in layers till all ingredients are in the dish. Then put in a cup of meat stock and a cup of tomato sauce and put the dish into a hot oven to cook until the sauce has reduced. Now stir the yolk of an egg into a $\frac{1}{4}$ pint of cream and pour it on top of the Moussaka. Put the dish back in the oven to complete the cooking (about 20 minutes) and serve piping hot. The egg and cream form a kind of custard on the top of the Moussaka, about $\frac{1}{2}$ an inch thick; it should be golden brown.

This is a good dish for a large country luncheon party.

Elizabeth David.

Puddings Cold.

CHOCOLATE AND ORANGE MOUSSE

6 ozs. plain block chocolate	$\frac{1}{4}$ oz. (1 teaspoon) gelatine
$\frac{1}{2}$ gill water	juice of 1 orange
3 eggs	$\frac{1}{2}$ gill cream
2 egg yolks	
$2\frac{1}{2}$ ozs. castor sugar	

To Finish

2 tablespoonfuls ground hazelnuts	thinly sliced candied orange peel
a little whipped cream	

Melt the chocolate with the water to form a thick cream. Whisk the eggs, egg yolks and sugar together in a basin over hot water until thick. Remove from the heat and continue to whisk until the bowl is cold, then add the warm chocolate. Dissolve the gelatine in the orange juice over heat and add to the mousse. Stir until thickening, then fold in the partially whipped cream. Turn at once into a prepared soufflé case or glass bowl. When set, decorate with the ground nuts, candied peel and cream.

The Cordon Bleu School of Cookery.

Chocolate Marvel

Ambassador 4321.

15. Connaught Square,
London,
W. 2.

4 oz. plain chocolate
4 eggs.

Melt chocolate. Stir in yolks.
Beat whites well.
Add chocolate mixture carefully
to whites. Leave for 12 hrs, after
having turned into glass dish to set.

Lady Elizabeth von Hofmannsthal.

Strachur House,
Argyll.
Tel. Strachur 242.

COEUR À LA CREME

one large size cottage cheese   ½ pint cream
1 jar "Hero" black morello cherry jam

Whip ½ the cream and combine with cheese - press
into an oiled mould (heart-shaped if possible) - set
in fridge to chill - Before serving turn out into glass
dish, pour over the rest of cream (unwhipped) and serve
with the just heated cherry jam which has been slightly
diluted with water and a little kirsh liqueur in another
glass bowl.

Crème Brulée

Enough for 4 people

Yolk of 5 eggs, one pint
cream, put yokes &
cream into saucepan
add a little sugar.
Set in a pan of boiling
water until it sets, whisking
all the time. Pour into a
soufflé dish when cold &
lightly set. Put castor sugar
over the top & brown with
a salamander -

Mrs. Tony Keswick.

Strachur House,
Argyll.
Tel. Strachur 242.

HAZELNUT MERINGUE CAKE

4 egg whites
9 ozs. castor sugar
vanilla essence
½ teaspoonful vinegar
4½ ozs. browned ground
hazelnuts

½ pint cream, lightly
whipped
icing sugar and
raspberries to finish

Whisk the egg whites until stiff, then gradually beat in
the castor sugar and continue to beat until really stiff,
adding the vanilla and vinegar. Lastly fold in the slightly
toasted hazelnuts.   Fill into two 8-inch prepared
sandwich tins and bake for about 30 to 40 minutes in a
moderate oven, Reg. 5 or 375°F.   When cool, fill with
whipped cream, dust the top with icing sugar and hand
raspberries in a Melba sauce separately.

Melba Sauce

1 lb. raspberries   5 large tablespoonfuls icing sugar

Sieve about three-quarters of the raspberries. Work the
icing sugar into the purée by degrees, adding a little
more if necessary to sweeten nicely.   Then stir in the
reserved raspberries.

The Cordon Bleu School of Cookery.

Mont Blanc.

Pass ½ lb of cottage cheese through a sieve, or blender; whip ¼ pint of cream, and a tablespoonful of honey into the cheese. Continue whipping (or put into mixer) for 10 minutes. Chill. Peel & cook 1 lb of chestnuts, sieve or blend, shape into a pyramid and pour cream cheese over it.

A 1 lb tin of crème de marron can be used for this instead of the fresh chestnuts.

Viscountess Cranborne.

Monte Bianco — Another version —

1 lb chestnuts   pinch of salt
4 ozs icing sugar, sifted $\frac{1}{4}$ pint double cream
                Marrons glacé to decorate —

Make criss-cross slits on the skins of each
chestnut with a sharp knife — Cover them with
water and boil gently for 15 minutes — While
still hot remove shells & inner skins — Then
cover the shelled chestnuts with water and
simmer for 45 minutes — 1 hour, until very
soft — Drain thoroughly, mash in a bowl,
add sugar and salt and beat until smooth —
Then force the purée through a potato-ricer
on to the serving dish so that it forms a
cone-shaped mound of chestnut vermicelli.
Chill — Shortly before serving whip cream until
thick and heap over chestnuts until they are
completely covered — Decorate base with marrons glacé.

NORWEGIAN CREAM

$\frac{1}{4}$ oz. gelatine	$\frac{1}{2}$ teaspoonful vanilla essence
2 eggs	2 tablespoonfuls raspberry jam
4 ozs. castor sugar	$\frac{1}{4}$-pint cream

Dissolve $\frac{1}{4}$ oz. gelatine in $\frac{3}{4}$ teacupful cold water in a basin placed over a pan of hot water.   Separate whites from yolks of two eggs, add to yolks 4 ozs. castor sugar, $\frac{1}{2}$ teaspoonful vanilla essence and the melted gelatine. Beat until high up in the basin (or mixer).   Now fold in stiffly whisked egg whites.   Pour mousse into a glass dish and when cold spread a thin layer of raspberry jam, which has been reduced by boiling with a little water, and strained through a sieve.   Cover with whipped cream.

NUN'S PUDDING

4 eggs	4 leaves of gelatine
$\frac{1}{2}$ pint cream	$\frac{1}{2}$ pint milk
2 teaspoonfuls Cinnamon	2 tablespoonfuls apricot jam

Make the custard with the milk and 4 yolks of eggs.   Add 4 leaves of melted gelatine.   Pour into the dish into which it is going to be served and let it set.   Mix dessertspoonful of water with the jam.   Spread over custard.   Sprinkle cinnamon over jam.   Finish with thick layer of whipped cream.

This is a very old pudding and I think the name originates from the fact that it tastes vaguely like incense.

BROWN BREAD PUDDING

½ pint whipped cream
2 leaves gelatine *
2 whites of eggs
    little brandy or vanilla essence

1 heaped tablespoon of brown
breadcrumbs browned in the oven
sugar

Beat white of eggs very stiff. Whip the cream and add three-quarters of it to the beaten whites, then the breadcrumbs, sugar and flavouring and lastly the melted gelatine. Turn into a mould. When set, turn out and decorate with rest of cream and serve with compote of oranges handed separately.

* 2 leaves of gelatine = just over ¼ oz of the powdered kind.
                                     V.M.

COLD ORANGE SOUFFLÉ

5 oranges
1 lemon
5 eggs

5 tablespoonfuls sugar
1 packet Chivers orange jelly
a little cream

Squeeze the juice of five oranges and one lemon. Grate the skins of two oranges. Loosen the gratings in a little juice before adding to rest. Beat five egg yolks and five level tablespoonfuls of sugar in a mixer till sugar melts. Add the juice of the oranges. Go on beating. Meanwhile dissolve jelly in half a pint of boiling water. When cool,* add to mousse in mixer, still beating. Lastly, fold in stiffly beaten whites and pour into a glass dish. Decorate with skinned slices of orange and a little whipped cream.
It is better eaten next day.

* Really cool, otherwise mixture will seperate -
                                    V.M.

Hole of Ellel, Cark-in-Cartmel,
Lancashire.

ORANGE DESSERT

Oranges may be soaked in cold water for 24
hours.   6 bitter Seville Oranges cut in quarters.

Cook very slowly in syrup for several hours
until tender.   If necessary reduce the syrup to
a marmalade consistency.   Serve the quartered
oranges in the syrup cold.   Serve with Petit
Suisses or cream cheese.   Tangerines may be
substituted if desired.

Note:-

I found the skin of Scottish Seville
Oranges too tough - and next time I
made this delicious and very unusual
dish I sliced the oranges into circles.
Not so pretty, but safer.

V.M.

The Hon. Mrs. Ian Campbell-Gray.

Orange Jelly

Half a pound loaf sugar
18 oranges
2 lemons
1 oz. gelatine

Boil the sugar to a syrup, pour it boiling hot over the thinly peeled rind of two oranges. Pass through a silk sieve, add the dissolved gelatine & the syrup & a few drops of cochineal, and serve, not moulded, in a glass bowl. Serve with the jelly a dish of fresh compôte of oranges, all pips & pith removed and a hot syrup of sugar & juice poured over & allowed to cool.

Lady McEwen.

ORANGE PENNYMORE

6 oranges

3oz. almonds

1oz. candy peel

1 wine glass of orange curaçao (or brandy)

Skin the almonds and shred into thin strips.
Peel the oranges.   (This is the tiresome bit.   The
easiest way I've found is to have a dangerously sharp knife;
slice off both ends, stand one end on a chopping board, hold it
steady with a fork in the top end and slice the skin off
downwards in strips.   Very important to leave no pith.)
Cut the oranges into thin round slices and put a layer of
these into a bowl.   Sprinkle on some of the candy peel and
almonds.   Cover with another layer of oranges, candy peel
and almonds, and another, if there are any more.   Pour over
the orange curaçao.   Nicer if left in the Frig. for half an
hour before one eats it.

For 6 people.

Mrs. Richard Brooman-White.

Pamplemousse rafraîchi au champagne.

Grapefruit sections
Melon balls (preferably Honeydew or Persian)
Peeled green grapes

Marinade
~~Marinate~~ these for 1/2 hour – 1 hour in sugar and
a little Champagne. Chill slightly, after having added a little
chopped mint leaves.
Put into hollowed half grapefruits.
Add more champagne just before serving.

The Duchess of Argyll.

RICE CREAM

1 pint of milk	6 - 8 people
2 ozs. whole rice	
1 teaspoon vanilla essence	Compote of Rasperries
$\frac{1}{4}$ oz. gelatine	fresh or frozen
$\frac{1}{2}$ pint whipped cream	
2 ozs. castor sugar	

Boil the rice for 20 minutes in the milk with sugar added
when nearly ready - Take off fire and add melted gelatine
and vanilla essence - Leave to cool - when cold fold in
whipped cream - set in fridge - Serve with compote of
rasperries, or raspberries and redcurrants handed
separately.

SCHMIDT'S FRUIT FLAN

This is a very special flan that looks marvellous for
cold lunches or parties - It consists of a layer of thin
shortbread - on top of this a thin layer of very light
sponge cake, on top of which a lot of fruit is piled,
and then edged with a border of split bananas.   The
fruit is covered by a thin jelly made from the juices
of the fruit used - and then the whole pudding is covered
in whipped cream

The Shortbread Base

4 ozs. flour (plain)   3 ozs. margarine or butter
                 2 ozs. sugar

Mix all together - roll out thinly - about the thickness
of a $\frac{1}{2}$ crown - bake in a slow oven till biscuit coloured -
Cut while still warm to round shape.

Any favourite sponge mixture will do - this should not be
more than $\frac{1}{2}$" high.

Strawberries, raspberries, dried apricots, pears,
redcurrants, peaches or all suitable fruits - are better
if fresh - Bananas are essential for the border of flan.

STONE CREAM

This is a very old Lancashire dish.   You need a
step-ladder in the kitchen to make it and a lot of
newspaper on the floor.

1 pint cream	3 tablespoonfuls apricot jam
1 leaf gelatine	a wineglass sherry medium dry
a few drops vanilla essence	1 lemon

Boil 1 pint of good cream for a few minutes with a little
sugar, the melted gelatine and a few drops of vanilla or
ratafia essence.   Have ready a deep glass dish, cover
the bottom with apricot jam, a wineglassful sherry, the
juice of a lemon, and a little grated lemon peel.   When
the cream has cooled a little, pour it into this dish from
as high as you can.   Let it stand overnight in a cool place
before using.   In the morning the cream will be all bubbly
and aerated.

Scotch Trifle

3 small sponge cakes
6 macaroons
1 oz ratafias
¼ pint cooking sherry
3 tablespoonfuls brandy
little grated lemon rind

1 oz almonds
strawberry jam
¼ pint egg custard
freshly made whip
crystallised fruits
for garnish

method

Place sponges macaroons and ratafias in dish. Mix sherry and brandy and pour over them. Over this put lemon rind - almonds blanched and cut into strips - and a layer of jam. When custard is cool pour over the trifle. When cold heap whip lightly over top and garnish with fruits.

Whip

¼ pint cream
¾ oz sugar

1 egg white
1 teaspoonful cooking sherry

Whisk all together until bulk is nearly doubled.

A M Cameron.

Mrs. A. D. Cameron.

10 Warwick Avenue
W. 2

BLACKCURRANT LEAF ICE

An amusing white water ice that on a warm spring day will
cause uninitiated guests to wonder from where comes the
fragrant taste, is made of young blackcurrant leaves picked
long before the fruit appears.   Were it porphyry purple
they would be in no doubt of its origin.

Throw a large fistfull of the leaves into a pan of boiling
syrup ($\frac{1}{2}$lb. white sugar to a pint of water).   Cover and
allow to cool for 2 or 3 hours.   Strain and add the juice
of 6 (?) lemons.   Freeze in the usual manner.   Serve this
intriguing sorbet in glasses with a sprig of mint and
some crisp langue-de-chats.

Diana Cooper

Lady Diana Cooper.

Strachur House,
Argyll.
Tel. Strachur 242.

BANANA CREAM

For 4 people.

The invention of this dish is a combined effort
by Lady Lloyd and myself.   I started the idea and
she improved on it.   It is really a glorified
nursery pudding, but it is very good and can be
made in 10 minutes.

        6 Bananas.
        ½ pint Cream.
        2 tablespoonsful dark Barbados
                                Sugar.

Chop bananas roughly.   Combine with stiffly whipped
cream.   Pour into shallow fireproof dish.   Sprinkle
thickly with dark Barbados (foot) sugar and put under
the grill for a minute or two until sugar has just
melted.

'Foot' sugar can be obtained from all good grocers.
It is supposed to be the scrapings from the bottom
of sugar barrels that Barbadians scrape together
with their feet!

'Monkhopton' Mocha Pudding.

First, make a Victoria Sponge sandwich (2 eggs)

Filling.
  2 egg yolks
  2 oz caster sugar
  4 " butter
  'instant' coffee (dry) to taste

Cream butter & sugar, add egg yolks & flavour to taste with the coffee.

Grease a bowl & fill it with layers of sponge & the filling, starting with sponge, & pressing down fairly hard. Leave overnight. Turn out & cover with remains of the filling & whipped cream.

Enough for 6 people.

Mrs. Richard de la Mare.

PORTSONACHAN.

BY DALMALLY.

ARGYLL.

DANISH APPLE CAKE

    1 lb. tart cooking Apples.
    8 oz. fresh Breadcrumbs, made from
                       a brown loaf.
    8 oz. Butter.
    8 oz. moist Brown Sugar.
    Redcurrant Jelly.
    Whipped Cream.

Spread the breadcrumbs on a baking tray, cover with
the sugar and dot with butter and put into a moderate
to hot oven, turning frequently until the sugar is
melted and the crumbs nicely browned. Meanwhile,
cut the apples and put them in a stew pan with very
little water, when soft put them through a fine
vegetable 'Moule'. Now put a layer of apples in a
glass dish, cover with a thin layer of redcurrant
jelly, and then the breadcrumbs. Repeat, and finish
the final layer of breadcrumbs with whipped cream.

Mrs. James Young.

PORTSONACHAN,

BY DALMALLY,

ARGYLL.

RUM AND RAISIN ICE CREAM

Basic Ice Cream

       6 Eggs.
       Vanilla Essence.
       1 pint Milk.
       ½ pint Cream.
       6 oz. Sugar.
       4 oz. Raisins.
       A measure of Rum.

Separate the yolks from the whites. Beat the yolks
with the sugar until thoroughly blended and lemon
colour, add the milk, the vanilla essence and the
lightly whipped cream, put in the freezing tray of
the **refrigerator** at least 5 hours before required.
Now soak the raisins in the rum. Half an hour before serving whip the egg whites, and add the raisins
and rum to the frozen mixture, blend thoroughly and
return to freezing tray until required.

Mrs. James Young.

LEMON CHEESE TARTLETS

2 large lemons   ½ lb lump sugar
3 oz butter   3 eggs

Melt the butter in a saucepan, then add the juice of

two lemons and the finely grated rind of one.

Beat the eggs well and stir them in carefully; continue

stirring until the mixture thickens, take off the fire and

beat well.   When cold put into very light puff pastry

tartlets and serve.   Only use the lemon cheese when it

has been freshly made.

Lady Jekyll

APRICOT PURÉE

1½ lbs dried apricots	1 small tin canned apricots OR
Sugar to taste	¾ lbs fresh peeled apricots
¼ pint cream	a few pistachio nuts

Soak 1½ lbs large dried apricots for 24 hours.

Simmer them in a little of the water they have been soaking

in until they are soft; then add either a small tin of

canned apricots or a few fresh peeled and stoned apricots;

boil together and if necessary sweeten a little and reduce.

Pass through a wire sieve or whirl in the liquidiser.

Serve in a glass bowl or in individual white china ramekin

dishes with a layer of thinly whipped cream covering the

puree and a few pale green peeled pistachio nuts sprinkled

on top.

Mrs. Charles Maclean

COFFEE MOUSSE

1½ - 2 pints of Whipped Cream.
1 cup of Sugar.
2 cups of very strong Coffee.
2 Eggs.
A very small pinch of Salt.

Melt the sugar and salt in cold coffee.

Beat the cream until it is stiff.

Add the sugar and coffee mixture slowly.

Beat in the two raw eggs and Freeze in deep freeze

or ice tray.

If liked, a sprinkling of newly ground coffee and
brown demerara sugar can be shaken over this pudding.

Lady Birley.

THE BYCULLA SOUFFLÉ

This is a very Edwardian dish; it was the pride
of the Byculla Club in Bombay, and in it's taste and
appearance are echoes of the British Raj. Mrs. Hawksby
and Mrs. Vansuythen may well have savoured it before
an afternoon at the races.

I have only the vaguest of recipes but plenty of
explanations on how to get the desired result: an
iced liqueur mousse in three differently coloured and
flavoured layers - Green Chartreuse, Benedictine and
Maraschine.   They are supposed to find their own (and
different) levels because of their specific gravity,
but, of course, they don't, because of the gelatine.

If anyone wants to make this rather cloying and de-
finitely intoxicating pudding for a dinner party of
Old Poona Colonels and their mem-sahibs, this is how
they should go about it:

    8 ozs. Cream.
    3 Eggs.
    2 oz. Sugar.
    Powdered Ratafia or any sweet biscuit.
    3 ozs. Milk.
    1 oz. Gelatine, melted in 1 tablespoon of
                        lemon juice or fresh lime.
    1 large liqueur glass Green Chartreuse.
    1 large liqueur glass Benedictine.
    1 large liqueur glass Maraschino.

Whisk together, or put in an electric mixer, the egg
yolks, sugar and milk.   Beat the egg whites separately
and add, then the stiffly whipped cream.   Divide the
mousse into three separate bowls and carefully fold a
different liqueru into each, having made the green
chartreuse darker with a few drops of green colouring,
and the maraschino pink with a few drops of cochineal.
Then add carefully, to each, a third of the gelatine

that has been melted in the lemon juice, having let
it cool a bit, but not set. Then immediately pile
the three mixtures into a large china souffle dish,
starting with the maraschino, then the benedictine,
then the chartreuse; smooth over the top and set in
an ice box for two hours. Before serving sprinkle
the top with crushed ratafias or any sweet biscuit.

Puddings Hot.

APPLE AND ORANGE TART

French Flan Pastry:

4 ozs. plain flour	2 ozs. butter
2 ozs. castor sugar	a few drops of vanilla
2 yolks	essence

Filling:

2 lbs. cooking apples	grated rind of 2 oranges
castor sugar	

To Finish:

2 seedless oranges	apricot glaze

First prepare the pastry. Sift the flour into a slab or board.
Make a well in the centre and in this put the rest of the
ingredients. Work up to a paste with the finger tips. Chill.
Roll out, fairly thinly, line into a flan ring, fill with paper
and rice and bake in the oven. Reg. 5 - 375 or 380°F.

Meanwhile prepare the filling - wipe, quarter and core the
apples, slice into a buttered pan. Cover lightly and cook to
a pulp. Sieve, return to the pan with the orange rind and 2 -
3 tablespoonfuls of sugar. Cook until thick, turn out and cool.

To Finish:

Turn this purée into the flan, smooth over the top, cut away
peel and pith from the oranges, slice into rounds arrange
them on top of the flan, and brush with apricot glaze.

The Cordon Bleu School of Cookery

Baked Bananas Créole (4 or 5 people)

Lay half a dozen peeled, ripe bananas in a shallow fire-proof dish, and sprinkle over them

3 Tablespoonfuls of brown sugar.

The juice of 1 lemon.

3 Tablespoonfuls of water.

Bake in a slow oven until the bananas are brown, adding, half way through the cooking

1 sherry-glassful of rum.

Serve with whipped cream handed separately.

Mrs. Christopher Soames.

Strachur House,
Argyll.
Tel. Strachur 242.

WHISKY BANANAS   for 4 people

6 bananas   2 tablespoonfuls butter
3 tablespoonfuls sugar   3 tablespoonfuls whisky

Fry bananas, skinned but whole, in butter with sugar
sprinkled over them. When sugar begins to caramelise
and bananas are well cooked, heat whisky in separate
saucepan. Set light to it and pour it over bananas. Serve
at once.

BLACKBERRY AND APPLE PIE

Everyone will know how to make this:

thickly sliced apples and blackberries in layers in a deep
pie dish, sprinkled with sugar, a suspicion of lemon rind,
and a rich short pastry top. Served hot with whipped cream -

but I do not hesitate to include it as it is one of the best
puddings in the world.

BROWN BETTY

2 large cups apple purée	1 teaspoonful ground cinnamon
1½ teacups breadcrumbs	1½ tablespoonfuls margarine
½ cup sugar	1 tablespoonful marmalade

boiling water

Place half the apple in a greased pie dish. Mix the crumbs with about ½ teacup fine granulated sugar and cinnamon, then sprinkle half of this over fruit. Dab with half the fat. Cover with remainder of fruit then with remainder of crumb mixture and dab with rest of fat. Sprinkle either with 2 tablespoonfuls grated orange rind or with 1 tablespoonful marmalade moistened with 1 tablespoonful boiling water and then 1/3 teacup cold water. Cover with plate. Put in moderate oven (375°F) and cook for ¾ hour.

PORTSONACHAN,

BY DALMALLY,

ARGYLL.

APPLE FLAN MONTARGIS

Large eating Apples.
8oz. Butter.
8oz. Sugar.

Pastry.
6 oz. Flour.
3 oz. Butter.
2 oz. Castor Sugar.
2 Egg Yolks.
A few drops Vanilla.

Take a shallow saute pan, over low heat melt the butter
and sugar and allow to caramelize.   Peel and core the
apples and cut in half.   Place them upright in the
saute pan, in circles until the pan is quite full,
cook carefully until butter and sugar is absorbed in the
apples, but they should remain firm.   Now make the
pastry as indicated and cover the apples.   Put in a
hot oven and bake 25 to 30 minutes.   When the pastry
is cooked, remove from oven and cool a little.   Now
turn out on to a large round plate with the pastry
underneath and the apples on top.   The apples should
be firm and nicely caramelized.

Mrs. James Young.

TREACLE TART

Make Pastry Case of:

$\frac{1}{2}$ lb. plain Flour.
$\frac{1}{4}$ lb. Butter.
2 tablespoons Cold Water.
2 level dessertspoons Sugar.
Salt-spoon Baking Powder.

Golden Syrup.
Fresh White breadcrumbs.
Squeeze of Lemon.

Rub butter into flour, until it looks like fine breadcrumbs , add sugar and baking powder, mix well, add
cold water (and if preferred yolk of egg).   Line
flan tin with pastry.   Cover bottom well with fresh
white breadcrumbs.   Cover these with golden syrup,
slightly warmed, and lemon juice.   Cover top like
latice work with trimmings of pastry.   Bake in a
fairly hot oven until pastry is cooked and golden
brown.

Crêpes soufflées au Grand Marnier

Make some sweetened pancakes. (The following soufflé mixture will fill about 16). Keep them between two plates. Put in a saucepan 3½ oz caster sugar, 1½ oz flour, 8 fluid oz of cold milk & 8 fluid oz of Grand Marnier. Mix up, bring to the boil, remove from fire and add, one by one, 6 egg yolks. Fold in the very stiff whites, fill the pancakes, roll up, arrange on a fireproof dish & bake in a moderate oven for 10 minutes.

Lady Shuckburgh

BEAUFORT CASTLE,
BEAULY,
SCOTLAND.

REGENCY PUDDING

4 dessertspoonsful Sugar
  for caramel
3 oz. sugar
1 lemon
5 eggs
¼ pint whipped cream
1 egg for sauce
3 oz. butter

Line a mould with caramel (see Hedgehog Pudding, page 185).
Put in a pan 3 oz. of butter, 3 oz. sugar, the thinly
peeled rind and juice of a lemon and 5 yolks. Beat
lightly over heat until like thick cream. It is best done
in a basin in a panful of hot water. Beat whites to a
stiff froth. Combine when yolks have cooled a little.
Pour into mould and steam for three-quarters of an hour.
The water around the mould must not boil. It should not
be higher than about 210°. Turn out on to shallow dish
and serve with whipped cream and a sauce made by putting
one egg and a little cream into the pan in which you have
made the caramel, heating and beating till frothy.

Gâteau en Surprise

Genoese cake cooked in a round mould. Take out the inside. Fill with stiffly whipped, unsweetened cream, pour hot chocolate over the whole.

Gâteau Egyptienne

The same as above, adding hot black-berry jelly instead of chocolate.

Lady McEwen.

GUARDS' PUDDING

5 ozs. breadcrumbs	3 tablespoonfuls home-
2 ozs. sugar	made strawberry jam
3 ozs. melted butter	1 teaspoonful bi-carb. of
2 eggs	soda.

Mix breadcrumbs, soda, sugar and jam together in a bowl.
Add melted butter, then well-beaten eggs. Turn into a
well-buttered basin, cover with greaseproof paper and
steam for $1\frac{1}{4}$ hours, making sure the water never goes off
the boil. Serve with hot strawberry jam and whipped cream
handed separately.

NORMANDY PUDDING

6 large peeled and cored apples	3 eggs
3 tablespoonfuls apricot jam	2 oz. sugar
4 ozs. breadcrumbs	a little butter
lemon juice	

Cut the apples in halves and cook in a shallow entree dish
in butter with the apricot jam and lemon and sugar spread
over them. Take out of oven and cool dish a little. Mix
4 ozs. breadcrumbs with butter crumbs and fry them in
clean pan. Pour over pie dish. Then take 3 eggs and
2 ozs. sugar and whip them over hot water (in a bowl over
a saucepan). *   When creamy, pour over apples and
crumbs and brown slightly in a slow oven.

* Can be done in electric mixer.

4, Hillside, Lancaster.

APPLE   AND   APRICOT   PUDDING

8 cooking apples   ½-can Australian whole apricot jam
                        1 lemon

    Greese a shallow entrée dish with butter.   Peel,
core and quarter 8 cooking apples.   Slice into ½-inch
thick quarters and lay neatly in rows down dish.   Cover
with apricot jam that has been loosened a bit with a
tablespoonful hot water.   Squeeze over the juice of
one lemon and sprinkle with a few bits of thin lemon
skin (the yellow outer skin).   Bake in oven till apple
is cooked.   About 15 minutes.

Mrs. L. Cowper.

HEDGEHOG PUDDING

For the pudding -

6 whites of eggs	enough sugar to maramelise
6 dessertspoonfuls sugar	the sides of a soufflé dish
pinch salt	½ cupful almonds

For the sauce   -

6 yolks of eggs	½ pint cream

Separate six whites of eggs from the yolks and beat them to a
stiff froth, adding a dessertspoonful of sugar for each egg
(as for meringues). Add a pinch of salt. Heap into a
caramelised soufflé dish and steam in a saucepan of water for
an hour and a half. The water round the dish must not boil.
Blanch half a cupful of almonds, split and brown slightly in
oven. Turn pudding out into a shallow glass dish. Stick almonds
all over it and serve with half the caramel sauce poured round
and half handed separately.

The Sauce

Beat the yolks separately until they are thick and creamy and
pour on to them half a pint of just boiling cream.

To Caramel a Soufflé Dish

Put 4 dessertspoonfuls of sugar into a frying pan and let them
melt slowly into a syrup.   Do not burn. When golden, pour
into soufflé dish and roll it round so that it covers the sides
and bottom.

LEMON SOUFFLÉ

This is a light and delicious end to a rich dinner menu.

4 eggs   the juice and rind of
3 tablespoonfuls castor sugar   one lemon

Beat the yolks of the eggs high with the sugar, the grated
rind of the lemon and the juice, for several minutes.
Whip the whites and fold them in.   Pour into a buttered
soufflé dish and cook for 10 - 12 minutes in a medium-hot
oven - about Regulo 7.

Soufflés made without the addition of flour are very light
and creamy, but the whole operation should be performed
with speed, and the exact heat of the oven and the timing
can only be learnt by experience.

Elizabeth David.

CROUTE d'ORE

1 Milky Loaf.

Soak rounds of bread in milk and then put
the bread in beaten egg with a pinch of
salt.   Fry the bread in clarified butter
until golden brown; sprinkle with cinammon
and icing sugar and place under grill for a
moment.   Serve with maple or golden syrup.
For extra richness also serve whipped cream.

The Hon. Mrs. Christopher Bridge.

Ambassador 4321.

15. Connaught Square.
London,
W. 2.

TOFFEE PUDDING

Cut the required number of pieces of white bread
into the size of playing cards 1" thick.

Dip in milk.

Meanwhile boil

2 oz. sugar
2 oz. butter
4 oz. golden syrup

to a light brown colour.   Fry bread lightly in
the mixture.   Pile on a hot dish.   Serve whipped
cream with this.

Lady Elizabeth von Hofmannsthal.

N.B.   My family always called this pudding 'Pain
        Perdu', as it was a good way of using up
        bread which would otherwise be 'lost'.

                                            V.M.

POMME   DEMEDOFF

First stew 6 apples.   When cold put them into
a shallow wide buttered fireproof dish.   Fill
apples with apricot jam & cover with the
following mixture.

Melt 1oz. of butter, stir in 1oz. of flour and add
1 gill of boiling milk.   Take off the fire and
mix in, 2 egg yolks the juice of $\frac{1}{4}$ lemon 2oz.
sugar and 2 stiffly beaten whites of egg.   Cook
in medium oven 350 for about 20 minutes.

Mrs. Ronald Foster.

Strachur House,
Argyll.
Tel. Strachur 242.

ZABAGLIONE

1 egg yolk	)	
1 dessertspoonful fine castor sugar	)	per person
1 dessertspoonful Marsala	)	

Beat the egg yolks and sugar in a bowl sitting in hot
water in a large pan over a moderate heat till it
begins to thicken, gradually add the Marsala and
keep on beating.   To give greater bulk (it lessens
the richness of this delicious pudding) you can add,
off the fire, half the whites of the eggs separately
beaten - I only advise this if it is to be made for more
then six people.   Pour into wine glasses or china
shells - and eat while still warm.

Scones & Cakes.

MRS. DUNCAN'S GIRDLE SCONES

½ lb. plain Flour.
1 good teaspoonful cream of Tarter.
½ teaspoonful baking Soda.
A good pinch coarse Salt.
Milk to mix.
A little Golden Syrup.

Sift all the dry ingredients through sieve into a
china bowl.   Make a well in the middle and pour in
enough milk (buttermilk is best) to make a loose and
slightly slippery dough.   Mix with a palette knife
and at the end dip the knife into a tin of golden
syrup so that just a little syrup coats it and is
mixed into the dough.

Turn out on to floured slab.   Roll out, using
rolling pin as little as possible and always rolling
away from you.   Cut into triangles or rounds and
cook on a hot but not roasting girdle that has been
lightly floured.

Mrs. Duncan Sinclair.

TREACLE SCONES

8 oz. plain Flour.
1 level teaspoonful Bicarbonate of Soda.
2 level teaspoonfuls Cream of Tartar.
½ level teaspoonful Ground Ginger.
½ level teaspoonful Ground Cinnamon.
¼ level teaspoonful Salt.
1 oz. Castor Sugar.
1½ oz. Margarine.
1 level tablespoonful Black Treacle.
Almost ¼ pint Milk.
A little extra Milk for the glaze.

Sift the flour, bicarbonate of soda, cream of tartar,
ground ginger, cinnamon and salt into a mixing bowl.
Add the sugar and rub in the margarine.
Melt the treacle in two tablespoonsful of the milk
then add to almost all the rest of the milk.   Make
a hollow in the centre of the dry ingredients, add
the treacle-flavoured milk and mix to a soft dough.
Add the rest of the milk only if it is required.
Turn the dough on to a floured board, knead it very
lightly into a round, and then put it on a floured
baking tray.   Mark the large scone into eight
sections with a knife then brush the surface with
milk.
Bake the scone in a hot oven, about Gas Mark 7 or
425 degrees, for ten to twelve minutes, then reduce
the heat to Gas Mark 4 or 355 degrees for a further
five minutes.   Cool the scones on a wire tray and
then break it into sections.

POTATO SCONES

1 lb. unpeeled Potatoes.
2 oz. Self-raising Flour.
½ level teaspoonful Salt.
1 oz. Butter.
Melted Butter to serve with Scones.

Boil potatoes until they are tender - then drain.
Dry well by tossing pan over heat and then rub through
sieve.

Sift the flour and salt together and rub in the butter.
Mix in the sieved potato and beat.   If dough is too
stiff add a little of the water potatoes have cooked
in.   Roll out into three rounds about 8" in diameter
and the thickness of a florin on a floured board or
marble slab.   Cut into portions like a cake.   Cook
both sides on a hot girdle that has been dusted with
flour.

Serve with melted butter in a hot muffin dish.   (Scones
can be kept in a tin and reheated).

Strachur House,
Argyll.
Tel. Strachur 242.

OATCAKES

$\frac{1}{2}$ lb. oatmeal $\frac{1}{2}$ teaspoonful baking soda
1 pinch of salt   1 dessertspoonful bacon fat

Mix all ingredients together with hot water - to a stiff and
not too wet dough.   Work well and quickly with your hands
and roll on to oatmealed baking board - about as thick as
a $\frac{1}{2}$ crown.   Cut into rounds and cook both sides on girdle
or alternatively on an oven sheet in the oven (you don't have
to turn them in oven).   They are ready when they are really
dried through.

BEAUFORT CASTLE,

BEAULY,

INVERNESS-SHIRE.

DOT'S OVEN SCONES

3 cups S.R. Flour
2 oz. margarine
2 teaspoonfuls baking powder
pinch salt
1 egg

Rub margarine into flour, add salt, & baking powder.
Beat egg with a little milk, mix into flour & add
enough milk to make a soft dough. Turn onto
floured board & roll out to $\frac{1}{2}$ inch. thickness.
Cut into rounds, put on baking sheet, and cook in
hot oven for 8 to 10 minutes.

Lady Lovat
(Miss Dorothy Fraser)

54, Queen's Gardens, London.

ICED GINGER SHORTBREAD

8 oz. butter
8 oz. flour

4 oz. castor sugar
2 small teaspoonfuls
ground ginger

Cream the butter and sugar; work in the flour sifted with ginger and knead until smooth and without cracks. Roll out on a floured board to about $\frac{1}{4}$ inch thick and bake at (Regulo 4) 350°F until pale golden brown. Remove from the oven and cut into small, neat pieces.

Cover with the following icing.

Ginger icing: Take 2 oz. of butter, 3 dessertspoonfuls of syrup, 8 tablespoonfuls of icing sugar, 2 small teaspoonfuls of ground ginger.

Melt the butter in a small saucepan, add the other ingredients, and bring slowly to the boil. Remove from heat, beat until thick, and spread with a hot knife on the shortbread pieces.

Miss Jeanne Thomlinson.

Chocolate Cake

½ lb butter beaten to a cream.

7 egg yolks and whites beaten separately
The whites stirred in last.

½ lb bitter or vanilla chocolate scraped
down & heated in the oven, then beaten
into the butter with 3oz flour.

½ lb sifted sugar

4 oz pounded almonds

1 teaspoon of salvolatile.

This cake must be baked in a slow oven.
It is better when eaten two days old —
A thin icing of sugar keeps it moist.

The Duchess of Devonshire.

Strachur House,
Argyll.
Tel. Strachur 242.

CHOCOLATE BISCUIT CAKE

$\frac{1}{4}$ lb. each chocolate menier or Cadbury's Red Label cocoa sugar and margarine
1 egg

1 teaspoonful (exact) water
$\frac{1}{2}$ lb. crushed tea biscuits (rich tea are best)

Cream butter and sugar, add beaten egg, then chocolate, water and not too finely broken biscuits (about size of peanuts). Press well into a greased tin with loose bottom and leave for two days in a cool place. Ease round the sides with a knife. Turn out carefully and sprinkle with icing sugar or grated chocolate.

Trocadero Cake.

Ingredients.

4 ozs Self raising flour. 4 ozs margarine.
4 ozs Castor sugar. 1 Large tablespoonful
of home made marmalade. 2 eggs. 1
Tablespoonful of almost boiling water.

Cream margarine and sugar thoroughly.
Beat eggs together. Add gradually to the
creamed mixture, and stir in flour lightly.
Then add large tablespoonful of marmalade, and add water last of all.
Put into well greased sandwich tin
and bake in a moderate oven for 40
minutes.
When cool cover top of cake with another tablespoonful of marmalade.
Ice all over with white icing.

Mrs. Maclean of Ardgour
(Miss Ivy Weald)

RHODA'S WHISKY CAKE

7 oz. seedless raisins	1 egg
$\frac{3}{4}$ pint water	6 oz. plain flour
4 oz. cooking fat	1 level teaspoon bicarb. soda
5 oz. castor sugar	$\frac{3}{4}$ teaspoon ground cloves
4 oz. walnuts (chopped)	$\frac{3}{4}$ teaspoon nutmeg
2 tablespoonfuls whisky	1 pinch all spice
	1 teaspoon salt

Filling:-   14 oz. icing sugar, 1 small egg, 1 tablespoon
whisky, 2 oz. butter.

To make:

Grease and paper line two 9 in. sandwich tins. Cover raisins
with water and simmer 20 mins. Drain, saving one third
liquid.   Cool.   Cream fat and sugar together until light and
fluffy.   Beat in egg.   Sift together flour, spices, and salt.
Fold into mixture alternately with liquid. Stir in raisins,
nut and whisky. Pour into tins. Bake in moderate oven
(gas No. 4 - 350° electric) for 30-35 minutes. Cool on a wire
tray. Sandwich together with some of filling and spread rest
on top.

Filling: Cream butter and gradually beat in the icing sugar
alternately with lightly beaten egg and whisky.

Strachur House,
Argyll.
Tel. Strachur 242.

SLOVENIAN COFFEE CAKE (Tonshika's recipe)

The Cake

5 whole eggs
3½ ozs. flour
1½ tablespoonfuls cold water

5 tablespoonfuls sugar
saltspoonful baking powder

Beat the sugar and eggs together for 30 minutes (20 minutes in a mixer). Add slowly, beating all the time 1½ tablespoonfuls cold water. Continue beating for another 15 minutes. Add baking powder to flour and sieve all at once into eggs and sugar. Then only mix a minimum amount. Pour into a baking tin that has been well greased and floured and put into a hot oven (temp. 375°) for 25 minutes.

When cooked and cold, slice cake into three and spread layers with butter icing. Replace layers and completely cover with icing. Finish with walnut garnish.

The Icing

3½ ozs. sugar
2 tablespoonfuls cold water

1 whole egg
½ lb butter (unsalted)
coffee flavouring

Boil water and sugar together with a stick of vanilla. Beat up a whole egg in a bowl, and when sugar is thick remove

vanilla pod and pour on to beaten egg.   Continue whisking
and add bit by bit ½ lb chopped up saltless butter.

If it is difficult to mix, put the bowl in the oven for a
minute and then continue mixing with whisk.   Mix until cold
and thick and smooth, and then add very strong black coffee
to taste.

This icing can also be flavoured with orange or lemon juice
and grated rind for an orange or lemon cake.

WINTER GINGERBREAD CAKE

"- Black and sticky with treacle, enlivened by whole
white almonds -"

One pound of flour, 1 lb. black treacle, 1 dessertspoonful ground ginger, ½ lb. brown sugar, ½ lb. butter,
½ pint milk, ½ teaspoonful carbonate of soda, 4 eggs, a
little finely-chopped citron, and white almonds (whole)
for top.

Mix the dry ingredients together, warm the milk and
dissolve the butter in it, beat up the eggs, then add
treacle and stir into the dry ingredients, beat well,
bake ¾ hour.   This mixture should be a running consistency before baking, so add more milk if necessary.
Bake in a flat brick-shaped tin; or if preferred round
and deep, a saucepan will serve.

Lady Jekyll.

Brides' Slices.

4 ozs. Margarine.

4 ozs. Brown Sugar.

Cream, and add 2 eggs, 1 teaspoonful
mixed spice, 6 tablespoons cake crumbs
and 1 lb. currants.

Spread over $\frac{1}{2}$ lb. uncooked shortcrust
pastry and bake for 40 minutes in a
moderate oven.   Allow to cool.

Spread thin layer of marzipan on top
and coat with glacé icing.

Mrs. W. Henderson,
"St. Rule",
Ardrossan.

CARAMEL FINGERS

The Shortbread:
½ lb flour
4 oz butter (or margarine)
2 oz sugar.

Cream together butter and sugar and add flour.
Spread on tin, prick well and cook in oven till brown.
Put into a saucepan: 4 oz margarine, 2 tablespoons
Golden Syrup, 4 oz sugar and 1 small tin condensed milk.
Bring slowly to the boil and boil for five minutes.
Spread on top of the cooled shortbread. When cool
cover with melted chocolate (chocolate drops or black
chocolate melted with a little water) and cut into
fingers.

Given to me by Mrs. Davidson of Ardrossan, Ayrshire.

NOTES

NOTES

Savouries.

CORTACHY CASTLE
KIRRIEMUIR
ANGUS

CHEESE FLOAT   for 6 people

4 oz. grated Parmesan Cheese	$\frac{1}{2}$ pint cream
3 slices bread	pinch of salt
1 oz. butter	

Grease shallow ovenproof dish and cut bread in small rounds with scone cutter.   Place layer in bottom of dish and sprinkle with cheese.   Pour a little cream over bread just enough to soak in.   Place another layer of bread rounds on top and more cheese.   Now whip remaining cream and add 2 ozs. cheese to it.   Spread cream evenly over bread and sprinkle with remaining cheese and knobs of butter.   Put in moderate oven until brown on top.   Care must be taken not to have oven too hot as cream will overflow.   Serve very hot at once.

Lady Ogilvy
(Mrs. Chrissie Hanton)

WEMYSS CASTLE,

FIFE.

HOT   OR   COLD KISCH

Make a custard of 2 yolks & two whole eggs,
about a pint of milk & cream, then add three
ounces of grated Parmesan cheese.   Season
well with salt & pepper & a good dash of
cayenne pepper.
Steam in oven till just set.   If not brown
enough put under the grill for a second.

Lady Victoria Wemyss.

Mushrooms in Cream.

Ambassador 4321.

15. Connaught Square.
London,
W. 2.

Fry mushrooms (the flat ones if possible) in butter, place in fireproof dish. Put ¼ cream in a saucepan, salt and pepper, 1 dessertspoon Worchester sauce, boil to reduce (up to five mins:) Pour over mushrooms. Brown under grill.

Lady Elizabeth von Hofmannsthal.

BEAUFORT CASTLE,
BEAULY,
INVERNESS-SHIRE.

CRÈME LORRAINE

Fry two or three rashers of streaky bacon, and when very crisp break into small pieces.

Take ¼ lb. of grated cheese, (Gruyere and Parmesan mixed in equal parts) and ½ pint of cream, mix these togetherr and add one egg, well beaten, and the bits of bacon, a pinch of salt and of cayenne pepper.
Mix well and pour into individual souffle or ramekin dishes.   Cook carefully in bain marie in a fairly hot oven.

Serve with hot fingers of toast.

Lady Lovat
(Miss Dorothy Fraser).

PARMESAN WAFERS

6 Fingers Bread.
Cream.
Grated Parmesan Cheese.

Soak the bread in the cream, coat with grated cheese,
fry quickly in deep fat or brown in the oven.

Mrs. James Young.

      *   *   *

LAITANCES AU VIN BLANC

Arrange some large soft roes in a buttered fire-proof
dish.   Tinned ones will do quite well.   Season well
with salt, pepper, and lemon juice; add half a glass
of dry white wine and a few shavings of lemon rind;
sprinkle the top with browned bread crumbs and a few
crumbs of butter.   Cook for a few minutes on the top
shelf of the oven or under a hot grill.

PRUNES AND CHUTNEY   for 4 people

6 prunes   6 rashers bacon
1 hard-boiled egg   6 rounds thin bread
1 tablespoonful chutney

Soak prunes overnight and stew gently.   When cold -
stone and remove most of pulp.   Mix this with chopped
hard-boiled egg and chopped chutney.   Restuff prune
with this.   Wrap in a rasher of bacon.   Secure with
toothpick and fry in butter.   Serve on fried croûtons of
bread.

PORTUGUESE EGGS   for 4 - 6 people

Sweat a chopped onion in butter in a saucepan.   Add 2
skinned and chopped tomatoes.   Season well and add
one teaspoon of curry powder (Vencata Chellum).
Break 5 eggs into this and scramble gently.   Serve on
rounds of hot buttered toast.

Odds & Ends.

BAKED BEANS

Soak overnight in cold water white or brown haricot
beans.   Cook in boiling salted water until tender - drain
and put in deep fireproof dish with a cover (cast iron is
best) add one can good italian tomato purée, a little onion
juice (or 1 clove garlic) some green bacon and cook for
2 hours in slow oven.

Serve in same dish with grilled rashers of streaky
bacon cut at No.3.

GERMAN CABBAGE

Shred a red or white cabbage - wash well and discard
hard bits - put in an iron saucepan with 2 tablespoons wine
vinegar, 3 rashers of bacon, pepper & salt, mix, and cook
with lid on for $1\frac{1}{2}$ hours until tender.   Drain off all juice
chop bacon up with cabbage and serve.

Lady McEwen.

CABBAGE AU GRATIN

Cook cabbage by steaming with ½ cupful of water for 10
minutes in a pan with lid on. Drain well and chop cabbage
on a board. Fry some rashers of streaky bacon and chop,
mix with cabbage and put in greased earthenware dish.

Make ½ pint of good béchamel sauce and pour over cabbage,
dot with butter crumbs and grated cheddar cheese. Brown
in oven (15 minutes).

CABBAGE CAKES

Proceed as above, but squeeze out as much moisture as
possible, then make little patties of the chopped cabbage
and bacon, roll carefully in flour and fry in bacon fat
till both sides are golden brown.

POTATO PATTIES

Left over mashed potatoes make delicious flat patties,
rolled in flour, both sides and edges, and then fried in
a very little good dripping or bacon fat. They will not
form a golden skin unless there is very little fat in the
pan. Turn carefully.

Very nice for a simple cold meat supper with a good green
salad.

TATTIES WITH CROWDIE

This is a seasonal treat and should only be eaten once
or twice a year when home-grown potatoes are new and
still an excitement. They should not be too small and
the floury mid-season kind like Arran Wonder are the
best.

Scrub and boil 3 lbs. of good young potatoes in their
skins until cooked (about 20 minutes). Only add salt
when water comes to the boil. When cooked drain and
shake over fire until all water has dried up. Serve in
a soup tureen or casserole with a large lump of butter
and a tablespoonful of finely chopped dill scattered over.
Accompany with a dish of home-made crowdie - or if this is
not a rich enough cheese for your palate, a good fresh
double cream cheese - like Mascarpone.

This is a main dish, and you won't want to eat much
afterwards except fruit or a cold fruity pudding.

Crowdie

Heat through a large pan of sour milk - when curd begins
to rise and break push to the side of stove and leave to
cool. Drain off whey by hanging in a muslin. Beat a
little fresh cream or butter into the curds, salt, pepper,
and if liked, a few chopped chives can be added.

Leek Salad

WEMYSS CASTLE,

FIFE.

For this small & Navy
then leeks are required.
Wash & clean in the
usual way then tie in
bundles & boil in Salted
water = drain well.
For the dressing —
Salt — pepper 2 tablesp. Salad
oil.
1/2 salt sp. mustard
1 teasp. Vinegar
1/2 " Sugar Dash of tarragon
Vinegar
mix all together & pour over
leeks when cold —

Lady Victoria Wemyss.

COLE SLAW DRESSING

(Suitable for shredded cabbage, chopped celery and
apple or cold potato salads)

1 Dessert spoon Sugar.
1 Dessert spoon Flour.
1 teaspoon Mustard.
1 teaspoon salt.
Few grains of Cayenne.
1 teaspoon Butter.
Yolk of 1 Egg.
⅓ cup Vinegar.
½ cup thick cream – sour (or sweet
                     if preferred)

Mix dry ingredients and mustard. Add butter, egg
and vinegar. Cook over boiling water, stirring till
mixture thickens. Cool, add cream and beat thoroughly.

     *   *   *

SAUCE FOR COLD MEAT

Make a vinaigrette sauce from 8 tablespoonfuls
olive oil, 2 tablespoonfuls Wine Vinegar, salt,
black pepper, a tablespoonful each of finely chopped
onion and parsley and a tablespoonful of capers.
Add two chopped hard-boiled eggs and lemon juice
to taste.

PORTSONACHAN,

BY DALMALLY,

ARGYLL.

HOLLANDAISE SAUCE

This is a classic sauce and is delicious with hot
salmon.   It curdles easily but this can be avoided
by adding a teaspoon of arrowroot.

>   3 tablespoons of Wine Vinegar.
>   6 Pepper Corns.
>   Bay leaf.
>   1 small teaspoon arrowroot.
>   4 oz. Butter.
>   2 Egg Yolks.
>   Seasoning.
>   Lemon Juice.

Put the vinegar, pepper corns and bay leaf into a
pan and reduce to a dessertspoon.   Set on one side.
Beat the egg yolks with a teaspoon of arrowroot, add
the vinegar and work in a small nut of butter and a
pinch of salt.   Set the bowl in a bain-marie over
gentle heat.   With a wooden spoon work the yolks
until thick, then add the softened butter bit by
bit as the sauce thickens, talking the bowl off the
heat if it thickens too quickly.   When all is added
season lightly and add a little lemon juice.   It
should be lightly piquant, and lukewarm rather than
hot.

Mrs. James Young's version, as it is so clear to
follow.

BÉARNAISE SAUCE

4 tablespoons Wine Vinegar.
6 Peppercorns, Bay leaf, Tarragon and
                                Chervil.
1 small chopped Shallot.
2 egg yolks.
1 teaspoon Arrowroot.

3 oz. Butter softened and an extra
        nut of Butter.

A piece of meat glaze, the size of a
        hazel nut or a salt spoon of Bovril.

Proceed exactly the same as for Hollandaise, adding
the meat glaze finally.

        *   *   *

MUSHROOM SAUCE

(for use with roast or grilled
            steaks)

Stew some sliced mushrooms (about ¼ lb.) in butter
in a saucepan with a lid on.   When tender add a
tablespoonful of Worcester Sauce.   Add a little gravy
from steaks and season well.   Cook for a few more
minutes.   Lastly add two tablespoonsful of cream.

V.M.

-224-

UNBOILED RASPBERRY JAM

1 lb. of Sugar to every 1 lb. of Fruit.

Put the sugar on sheets in the oven and let it get
thoroughly heated.   Meanwhile put the fruit into a
pan over the fire until it comes to boiling point.
When thoroughly heated, remove from the fire and
mash the fruit well into a pulp.   Then add the
sugar and stir or beat briskly for 5 minutes.
Cover and allow to stand for half an hour.   Then
beat again (5 mins) and leave for half-an-hour, and
beat another 5 mins (in all beating 15 mins).   When
it is ready put into jars and cover.

This jam looks and tastes wonderful - the colour is
a coraline scarlet - but like most things of beauty
it does not last and should be eaten before the New
Year.

The 'Grant' Loaf (Much Hadham version)
3 loaves.

1 3lb bag Prewitt's (or other) 100% wholemeal flour.

½ lb cracked wheat (from London Health Stores)
(or 3½ lbs flour).

1 oz yeast. 1 oz coarse salt. 1 oz brown sugar.
2½ pints warm water.

Warm flour, cracked wheat & salt in big bowl.
Warm yeast, brown sugar & ½ pt water in small
bowl till it becomes frothy. Whisk it up.
Pour into well in flour, add rest of the water
gradually & mix well. (Dough should be slippery)
Put into 3 well greased tins (they should be ½ full)
Allow to rise in a warm place or on a hot plate till
¾ full. Bake ½ hour in moderate oven & 20 min more in hot
one.

Mrs. Richard de la Mare

ENGLISH AND AMERICAN EQUIVALENT MEASURES

The English Imperial Pint = 20 liquid ounces

The American = 16 liquid ounces

The standard English measuring cup holds half a
    pint (10 liquid ounces).

When measuring dry ingredients in a cup, the avoir-
dupois weight will of course vary.   Here are a few
equivalents in American cups:

$\quad$ 1 lb flour = 4 cups sifted flour

$\quad$ $\frac{1}{2}$ lb granulated or castor sugar = 1 cup

$\quad$ $\frac{1}{2}$ lb brown sugar = $1\frac{1}{4}$ cups

$\quad$ $\frac{1}{2}$ lb butter = 1 cup.

Index

SOUPS

14. Maggie's Oyster Stew — Colonel Michael Dunning-White
15. Leek and Potato Soup — Lady Maclean
16. Fish Soup — The Duchess of Devonshire
17. Green Pea Soup — Lady Maclean
    Cold Pea Soup — Lady Maclean
18. Mushroom Soup — Mrs. Franz Osborn
    (Miss Josephine Rüegg)
19. Nettle Soup — Mrs. N. Lancaster
20. Potage Crème Maize — Mrs. Stirling of Keir
    (Mrs. Alice Thomson)
21. Tomato Soup — Mrs. A.D. Cameron
22. Velouté de Chevreuil aux Marrons — The Duchess of Argyll
23. Vichyssoise — Lady Amabel Lindsay
24. Water Cress Soup — The Hon. Mrs. Michael Astor
25. Gaspacho — Lady Maclean
26. Consommé à l'Indienne — Lady Jekyll
    Clear Bortchok — Mrs. James Young
27. Tomato Soup with Orange — Mrs. James Young

HOT FIRST COURSE or SUPPER DISHES

30. Eggs with Peperonata — Mrs. Walter Smart
31. Mrs. Gibson's Egg Dish — Mrs. N. Lancaster
32. Frizzled Eggs — Lady Maclean
33. Eggs Steinbeck — Lady Maclean
    Egg and Mushroom — Lady Maclean
34. Mrs. Grady's Egg Dish — Lady Maclean
    Eggs in Black Butter — Lady Maclean
35. Egg Casserole à la Madras — The Hon. Mrs. Ian Campbell-Gray
36. Oeufs Mollets en Soufflé — Lady McEwen
37. Whiting and Tomato Soufflé — Lady Douglas-Home
38. Mexican Risotto — Lady Maclean
39. Mushrooms and Fromage — Mrs. Stirling of Keir
    (Mrs. Alice Thomson)
40. Oeufs Savoyarde — Lady Lovat (Miss Dorothy Fraser)
41. Oeufs Homefield — Lady Lovat (Miss Dorothy Fraser)
42. Green Omelette — Lady Peake (Tonshika)
43. Pâtés Vertes — The Hon. Mrs. Michael Astor

44.	"Sugo" for Spaghetti Bolognese	- Lady Maclean
45.	Spinach Roll	- Lady Peake (Tonshika)
46.	Swiss Eggs	- Mrs. Richard St. Clair de la Mare
47.	Tomato and Cauliflower au Gratin	- Lady Maclean
48.	Liver Kremoskies	- Lady Maclean
49.	Gnocchi Con Formaggio	- Lady Jekyll
50.	Imam Baildi	- Lady Maclean
51.	Risotto Alla Milanese	- Lady Maclean

COLD FIRST COURSE or SUPPER DISHES

54.	Chicken Liver Pâté	- The Lady Egremont
55.	Cold Cheese Soufflé	- The Hon. Mrs. Ian Campbell-Gray
56.	Smoked Salmon Mousse	- Mrs. V.F. Cavendish Bentinck
	Smoked Haddock Mousse	- Mrs. V.F. Cavendish Bentinck
57.	Melon à l'Anis	- The Hon. Mrs. Michael Astor
58.	Cold Crab Soufflé	- Lady Jekyll
59.	Venison Pâté	- Mrs. John Noble
60.	Pheasant Pâté	- Lady Sykes (Mrs. Scott)
61.	Stuffed Green Peppers	- Lady Maclean
	Salad Niçoise	- Lady Maclean
62.	Mousse of Tunny Fish	- Lady Maclean
63.	Ivar	- Lady Maclean

HORS D'OEUVRES

64.	Stuffed Hard Boiled Eggs	- Lady Maclean
	White Beans and Tunny Fish	- Lady Maclean
	Green Peppers Piedmontese	- Lady Maclean
65.	Chicken Livers	- Lady Maclean
	Raw Mushrooms	- Lady Maclean
	Cauliflower	- Lady Maclean
	Anchovy Fillets	- Lady Maclean
	Skinned Tomatoes	- Lady Maclean
	Smoked Dalmatian or Austrian Ham	- Lady Maclean
66.	Home Made Smoked Salmon	- Mrs. James Young
	Smoked Eel	- Lady Maclean
67.	Cold Sweet Corn	- Rhoda, Lady Birley
	Devilled Sardines	- Rhoda, Lady Birley

POULTRY and GAME

70.	Devilled Grouse	- Lady Ogilvy (Mrs. Chrissie Hanton)
71.	Grouse Salad	- Mrs. James Young
72.	Game Pie	- Lady Jekyll
73.	Devilled Turkey	- Lady Maclean
	Pheasant or Chicken Spatchcock	- Lady Maclean

74. Perdreaux a la Baretta   - Mrs. Stirling of Keir
                                                 (Mrs. Alice Thomson)
75. Roman Pie   - Lady Amabel Lindsay
76. Rhoda's Chicken Pilau   - Lady Maclean
77. Suprême Curzon   - Lady Amabel Lindsay
78. Casserole of Chicken   - Mrs. Franz Osborn
79. Kievski Kotelet   - Lady Maclean
80. Cold Chicken Lovat   - Lady Lovat (Miss Dorothy Fraser)
81. Iced Chicken Soufflé with
                  Curried Livers   - Lady Jekyll
82. Poulet à la Crème   - Lady Jekyll
      Paprika Stew   - Lady Jekyll
83. Barbecued Chicken   - Mrs. James Young
84. Petti Di Pollo Alla Bolognese   - Lady Maclean
85. Roast Duckling - Apple and
                   Raisin Stuffing   - Mrs. James Young
      Becassines Flambées   - Lady Jekyll
86. Joan's Rabbit Schnitzels   - Lady Maclean
87. Venison, Stewed in Red Wine   - Elizabeth David
88. German Receipt for Hare   - The Countess of Hardwicke

FISH

91. Sole au Gratin   - Lady Jekyll
      Oysters au Gratin   - Lady Jekyll
92. Cold Fillets of Sole with
                   Velouté Sauce   - The Hon. Mrs. Nigel Birch
93. Beaufort Sole with Oysters   - Lady Lovat (Miss Dorothy Fraser)
94. Haddock à la Crème   - The Hon. Mrs. Alan Hare
95. Haddock Pie   - Mrs. Richard Brooman-White
96. Halibut Strachur   - Lady Maclean
      Haddock Strachur   - Lady Maclean
97. Herrings in Oatmeal   - Lady Maclean
      Sole and Rice   - Lady Maclean
98. Truite à la Normande   - Lady Lloyd (Mrs. Wright)
99. Prawn or Shrimp Curry   - Lady Birley
100. Grilled Lobster   - The Duchess of Argyll
101. Lobster à la Newburg   - Lady Jekyll
102. Cod à la Portugaise   - Lady Maclean
103. Pauvre Homme   - Lady Maclean
104. Salmon Quiche   - Mrs. James Young
105. Baked Salmon   - Mrs. James Young
106. Coulibiac   - Mrs. John Noble
108. Dill Salmon or Trout   - Mrs. James Young

MEAT

112.	Oxtail	– Lady Lovat (Miss Dorothy Fraser)
113.	Boeuf Stroganov	– Lady Maclean
114.	Aiguillette de Boeuf Braisée	– Lady Shuckburgh
115.	Chicory and Ham Dish	– Miss Hübler
116.	Fillet of Roast Beef	– Mrs. A. D. Cameron
117.	Corned Beef Hash	– The Countess of Hardwicke
118.	Mrs. Bridgewater's Casserole	– Lady Maclean
119.	Pancake Cake	– The Hon. Mrs. Christopher Bridge
120.	Hot Pot	– Miss Hübler
121.	Rhoda's Shepherd's Pie	– Lady Maclean
	Rhoda's Brown Stew	– Lady Maclean
123.	Truffled Loin of Pork	– The Rt. Hon. Nigel Birch, M.P.
124.	Baked Ham with Honey Glaze	– Lady Birley
125.	Veal Escalopes or Pork Chops with Shura's Sauce	– Mrs. Shura Shihwarg
126.	Kidneys au Gratin	– Diana, Countess of Westmorland
127.	Paprika Goulash	– Cordon Bleu School of Cookery
128.	Pork Fillet with Cider and Lentil Purée	– Cordon Bleu School of Cookery
129.	Pork Fillet	– Mrs. Richard St. Clair de la Mare
130.	Barbary Lamb Stew	– Mrs. James Young
131.	Boiled Mutton with Caper Sauce	– Lady Lloyd (Mrs. Wright)
133.	Gigot of Lamb Poached in Milk	– Mrs. James Young
134.	Mutton Curry	– Lady Maclean
136.	Plov from Samarkand	– Sir Fitzroy Maclean
137.	Beyandi Kebab from Eskisehir	– Lady Maclean
138.	Ossobuco Fiorentine	– Miss Dolly Rae
140.	Veal Valentino	– Mrs. James Young
	Escalope of Veal à la Crème	– Mrs. James Young
141.	Escalope of Veal à la Marsala	– Lady Maclean
142.	Moussaka	– Elizabeth David

PUDDINGS – COLD

145.	Chocolate and Orange Mousse	– Cordon Bleu School of Cookery
146.	Chocolate Marvel	– Lady Elizabeth von Hofmannsthal
147.	Coeur à la Crème	– Lady Maclean
148.	Crème Brulée	– Mrs. Tony Keswick
149.	Hazelnut Meringue Cake	– Cordon Bleu School of Cookery
150.	Mont Blanc	– Viscountess Cranborne
151.	Monte Bianco	– Lady Maclean
152.	Norwegian Cream	– Lady Maclean
	Nun's Pudding	– Lady Maclean
153.	Brown Bread Pudding	– Lady Maclean
	Cold Orange Soufflé	– Lady Maclean
154.	Orange Dessert	– The Hon. Mrs. Ian Campbell-Gray

155. Orange Jelly	- Lady McEwen
156. Orange Pennymore	- Mrs. Richard Brooman-White
157. Pamplemousse Refraichi au Champagne	- The Duchess of Argyll
158. Rice Cream	- Lady Maclean
159. Schmidt's Fruit Flan	- Lady Maclean
160. Stone Cream	- Lady Maclean
161. Scotch Trifle	- Mrs. A. D. Cameron
162. Blackcurrant Leaf Ice	- Lady Diana Cooper
163. Banana Cream	- Lady Maclean
164. 'Monkhopton' Mocha Pudding	- Mrs. Richard de la Mare
165. Danish Apple Cake	- Mrs. James Young
166. Rum and Raisin Ice Cream	- Mrs. James Young
167. Lemon Cheese Tartlets	- Lady Jekyll
168. Apricot Purée	- Mrs. Charles Maclean
169. Coffee Mousse	- Lady Birley
170. The Byculla Soufflé	- Lady Maclean

PUDDINGS - HOT

174. Apple and Orange Tart	- Cordon Bleu School of Cookery
175. Baked Bananas Créole	- Mrs. Christopher Soames
176. Whisky Bananas	- Sir Fitzroy Maclean
Blackberry and Apple Pie	- Lady Maclean
177. Brown Betty	- Lady Maclean
178. Apple Flan Montargis	- Mrs. James Young
179. Treacle Tart	- Lady Maclean
180. Crêpes Soufflées au Grand Marnier	- Lady Shuckburgh
181. Regency Pudding	- Lady Maclean
182. Gâteau en Surprise	- Lady McEwen
Gâteau Egyptienne	- Lady McEwen
183. Guards' Pudding	- Lady Maclean
Normandy Pudding	- Lady Maclean
184. Apple and Apricot Pudding	- Mrs. L. Cowper
185. Hedgehog Pudding	- Lady Maclean
186. Lemon Soufflé	- Elizabeth David
187. Croute d'Ore	- The Hon. Mrs. Christopher Bridge
188. Toffee Pudding	- Lady Elizabeth von Hofmannsthal
189. Pomme Demedoff	- Mrs. Ronald Foster
190. Zabaglione	- Lady Maclean

SCONES AND CAKES

193. Mrs. Duncan's Girdle Scones	- Mrs. Duncan Sinclair
194. Treacle Scones	- Lady Maclean
195. Potato Scones	- Lady Maclean
196. Oatcakes	- Lady Maclean

197. Dot's Oven Scones	- Lady Lovat (Miss Dorothy Fraser)
198. Iced Ginger Shortbread	- Miss Jeanne Thomlinson
199. Chocolate Cake	- The Duchess of Devonshire
200. Chocolate Biscuit Cake	- Lady Maclean
201. Trocadero Cake	- Mrs. Maclean of Ardgour (Miss Ivy Weald)
202. Rhoda's Whisky Cake	- Lady Maclean
203. Slovenian Coffee Cake	- Lady Maclean
205. Winter Gingerbread Cake	- Lady Jekyll
206. Brides' Slices	- Mrs. W. Henderson
207. Caramel Fingers	- Mrs. Davidson of Ardrossan

SAVOURIES

210. Cheese Float	- Lady Ogilvy (Mrs. Chrissie Hanton)
211. Hot or Cold Kisch	- Lady Victoria Wemyss
212. Mushrooms in Cream	- Lady Elizabeth von Hofmannsthal
213. Crème Lorraine	- Lady Lovat (Miss Dorothy Fraser)
214. Parmesan Wafers	- Mrs. James Young
Laitances au Vin Blanc	- Lady Maclean
215. Prunes and Chutney	- Lady Maclean
Portuguese Eggs	- Lady Maclean

ODDS and ENDS

218. Baked Beans	- Lady McEwen
German Cabbage	- Lady McEwen
219. Cabbage au Gratin	- Lady Maclean
Cabbage Cakes	- Lady Maclean
Potato Patties	- Lady Maclean
220. Tatties with Crowdie	- Lady Maclean
221. Leek Salad	- Lady Victoria Wemyss
222. Cole Slaw Dressing	- Lady Maclean
Sauce for Cold Meat	- Lady Maclean
223. Hollandaise Sauce	- Mrs. James Young
224. Béarnaise Sauce	- Lady Maclean
Mushroom Sauce	- Lady Maclean
225. Unboiled Raspberry Jam	- Lady Maclean
226. The 'Grant' Loaf	- Mrs. Richard de la Mare

227. English and American Equivalent Measures